# The Catholic Children's BIBLE

## Leader Guide

saint mary's press

The publishing team included Gloria Shahin, editorial director; Joanna Dailey, editor and staff writer; and consulting writers Brian Singer-Towns, Rita Burns Senseman, and Mary Kathleen Glavich, SND. The activities for All Saints' Day, Advent, Feast of Our Lady of Guadalupe, Epiphany, Ordinary Time, Lent, and the Annunciation of Mary were written by Maureen Gallo. Prepress and manufacturing coordinated by the production departments of Saint Mary's Press.

Cover illustration by Nathan Hale

Printed in the United States of America

4211

ISBN 978-1-59982-042-2, print
ISBN 978-1-59982-115-3, e-book

# Contents

# Chapter 1

## Welcome!

Welcome to the Saint Mary's Press® *Catholic Children's Bible Leader Guide.* We hope that this guide will be your faithful companion as you lead your young elementary students toward a deeper understanding of God's Word in Scripture.

Throughout this leader guide, you will find practical ideas to enhance your teaching of Scripture. But, before we open this treasure box of ideas, it might be helpful to present the philosophy behind the teaching of Scripture as outlined in this guide, an overview of the chapters in this guide, and a simple and basic lesson plan that can be used for every Featured Story in *The Catholic Children's Bible.*

## The Featured Story Pages

This philosophy, as well as the accompanying lesson plan, follows the simple acronym PREP, which stands for **P**repare, **R**ead, **E**ducate, **P**ractice. Every Featured Story in *The Catholic Children's Bible* revolves around the following four principles:

### 1. In order to read and understand Scripture, children need preparation.

We are old enough to have heard many Scripture stories over and over again. Sometimes this familiarity can impede our understanding, if we are not open to new insights. But often our familiarity means that, knowing the elements of a particular story, we can go more deeply into its meaning.

Yet children often are hearing much of Scripture for the very first time. They are coming to it "cold," as it were. And with just one reading, with no preparation at all, the basic meaning of the stories does not sink in. Yet preparing the children requires preparation on your part as well.

#### *Preparation for Teacher*

This leader guide—and the following chapters in particular—can help you prepare to prepare the children for reading and understanding Scripture:

- Chapter 2: Why Read the Bible?—essential background for understanding the Sacred Scripture in God's plan

- Chapter 3: Biblical Literacy and the Teaching of Scripture—an exploration of the meaning of *biblical literacy* and its implications for teaching Scripture to children

- Chapter 4: Looking through the Saint Mary's Press® *Catholic Children's Bible*—an explanation of each feature of *The Catholic Children's Bible*

- Chapter 5: Helping Children to Navigate the Saint Mary's Press® *Catholic Children's Bible*—an explanation of the special features of *The Catholic Children's Bible* designed to help children become comfortable with finding and reading passages from Scripture

- Chapter 6: Characteristics of Second, Third, and Fourth Graders—information on the characteristics of younger elementary-age children and implications for understanding Scripture

- Chapter 7: Teaching Scripture to Children—practical teaching tips for the classroom session

## *Preparation for Children*

Ideas for directly preparing children to hear and understand Scripture are included in the following chapters:

- Chapter 8: Scriptural Prayer with Children—practical ideas for using Scripture in prayer with children

- Chapter 9: Breaking Open the Word—a section with practical strategies for teaching Scripture and a section with reproducible masters outlining methods for teaching popular Scripture stories

- Chapter 10: Scripture through the Year, in Prayer and Activities—a seasonal approach to Scripture, with handouts for major seasons and feasts of the Church as highlighted in the *Lectionary*, each with a prayer and ritual guide and each followed by a hands-on activity

## 2. Children can read Scripture.

*The Catholic Children's Bible* has been developed with the thought that children, with the proper preparation, can read Scripture without being limited to a paraphrase. As you teach a Scripture story, draw the children's attention to the Scripture passages of the story highlighted in the Featured Stories of *The Catholic Children's Bible*. Ask several volunteers to read the passages aloud. Congratulate and affirm the children for reading the actual Scripture from a real Bible.

## 3. Education is needed for understanding.

Education is the purpose of the Understand It! and Tell It! panels found on the pages of the Featured Stories. Because the Scripture passages are ancient writings from a culture very different from ours, these features are essential to adequately presenting Scripture to children.

## 4. *Practice* means living out the message of Scripture in Christian life.

The word *practice* in this sense means "doing." In fact, this word comes from *praxis*, a Greek word that monks in the early Church used to describe their rule of life. "What is your praxis?" they would ask one another. In other words, "How are you living your life?" The Live It! panel on the Featured Stories pages is particularly geared to bringing Scripture into the lives of elementary-aged students.

The last two chapters in this leader guide relate specifically to Christian life and practice:

- Chapter 11: Word and Sacrament: Preparing for the Sacraments of Christian Initiation and the Sacrament of Penance and Reconciliation—a compendium of popular Scripture stories presented in basal texts for the Sacraments, linked to Featured Stories in *The Catholic Children's Bible*

- Chapter 12: From Here to Home: Sharing Scripture with the Family—practical ideas for encouraging family participation and family education in reading and understanding Scripture

## A Short Lesson Plan

A sample lesson plan using all of the elements of the Featured Story pages in *The Catholic Children's Bible*, as well as supplementary materials and ideas from this leader guide, might look like this:

Opening Song

Opening Prayer (with reading of Scripture of the day from Featured Story pages)

Featured Story Pages: Understand It!, Live It!, Tell It!

Hands-on Activity

Closing Prayer

Within this simple structure, which follows the PREP formula, you will be offering your students the riches of Scripture that meet their needs for preparation, reading, education, and practice in Christian living.

# Chapter 2

## Why Read the Bible?

The *Catechism of the Catholic Church* tells us that the Church "forcefully and specifically exhorts all the Christian faithful . . . to learn 'the surpassing knowledge of Jesus Christ' (Philippians 3:8) by frequent reading of the divine Scriptures"[1] (133). But why is it important to be a frequent reader of the Bible? The answer to this question must take into account the divine nature of the Bible. The Bible is not just any book; it is unique among all books. So to answer the question, "Why read the Bible?" we must also answer the question, "What is the Bible?" We have several ways of describing the Bible's uniqueness, and each description gives us some insight into why it is important to read its pages.

## The Word of God

We often call the Bible the Word of God. But the Word of God is not limited to Sacred Scripture. In Pope Benedict XVI's apostolic exhortation *The Word of the Lord (Verbum Domini),* he describes the Word of God as a divine symphony, "a single word expressed in multiple ways" (7). We hear God's Word through the wonder and majesty of creation, we hear it through human reason and conscience, we hear it through the prophets of the Old Testament, we hear it through the teaching of the Apostles and their successors, and we hear it through the words of Scripture. And what is the single word expressed through these multiple voices? It is Jesus Christ.

Jesus Christ is the full manifestation of the Word of God (see John 1:1–14). Jesus said at the Last Supper, "Whoever has seen me has seen the Father" (verse 9). We can only know the fullness of God's love and his saving plan by coming to know Jesus Christ. So one important reason for reading the Bible is because it helps us get to know Jesus. "Ignorance of Scripture is ignorance of Christ" (Saint Jerome).

## One Mode of Divine Revelation

We also describe the Bible as one of the privileged modes of Divine Revelation. Christ charged the Apostles to "go, then, to all peoples everywhere and make them my disciples: baptize them in the name of the Father, the Son, and the Holy Spirit, and teach them to obey everything I have commanded you" (Matthew 28:19–20). Through the power of the Holy Spirit, the Apostles taught others the fullness of the divine truth that had been revealed to them, both orally and in writing. Today, through the popes and the bishops of the Church, this truth is passed on to us in two modes: Sacred Tradition and Sacred Scripture.

Because of this, we have confidence that through the words of Scripture God reveals himself to us in a unique and special way. This Revelation is not abstract or theoretical. When we read the Bible in faith, God touches our minds and our hearts. When we approach the words of Scripture prayerfully, the Holy Spirit gives us an intimate connection with our loving Creator. So another important reason for reading the Bible is because it leads to intimate communion with God.

## Divinely Inspired

Finally, we believe the Bible is divinely inspired. This means that ultimately God is the author of the Bible. The human authors were inspired by the Holy Spirit to put down in words the truth God wished to reveal for the sake of our salvation—that is, so that we might be restored to full communion with him. Most Christians understand this dimension of divine inspiration, but there is another dimension to divine inspiration that is frequently overlooked. The same Holy Spirit that inspired the original authors of the Bible's books also works within us when we read their words. Saint Jerome tells us, "We cannot come to an understanding of Scripture without the assistance of the Holy Spirit who inspired it" (*Verbum Domini*, 16).

So another reason to read the Bible is to give the Holy Spirit a chance to work in our lives. When we read Scripture, the Holy Spirit comforts us in our difficulties, challenges us to grow in holiness, and calls us to become more perfect disciples of our Lord and Savior, Jesus Christ. All the saints testify to this power of Scripture in their lives.

So why read the Bible? We do it in order to know Jesus Christ, to have an intimate relationship with God, and to allow the Holy Spirit to work in our lives. These are three pretty good reasons for being a frequent Bible reader! A love for Scripture, expressed in frequent reading of God's Word, is the legacy we are privileged to hand on to our children.

# Chapter 3

## Biblical Literacy and the Teaching of Scripture

As a teacher or catechist of Catholic children, you know the power that Scripture has to touch children's hearts and inspire their moral and spiritual lives. To remind us to draw upon this power in catechesis, the Church's teaching documents always call us to make the Bible an integral part of our ministry:

> Catechesis should take Sacred Scripture as its inspiration, its fundamental curriculum, and its end because it strengthens faith, nourishes the soul, and nurtures the spiritual life. (*National Directory for Catechesis,* p. 70)

> Likewise, the holy synod forcefully and specifically exhorts all the Christian faithful, especially those who live the religious life, to learn "the surpassing knowledge of Jesus Christ" (Phil 3:8) by frequent reading of the divine scriptures. (*Dei Verbum,* 25)

Through your catechetical ministry with children, you equip them with the essential knowledge and skills required for their lifelong journey of faith. When it comes to the Bible, you want to begin teaching the knowledge and skills that will help the children to ultimately become biblically literate adults. So let's start by describing biblically literate adults.

Biblically literate adults are comfortable in reading and using the Bible. They know how the books of the Bible are arranged and how to quickly and easily locate a specific book or passage. They have a solid understanding of the biblical story of salvation history. They are familiar with key people and events of salvation history and can tell how God's saving power worked through those people and events. These biblically literate adults understand that any book or passage from Scripture must be understood in its proper context. When reading the Bible, they consider things like the literary genre, the culture of the time, the original author's intended message, how the message fits into the bigger picture of salvation history, and how the passage is understood in the Church's Tradition.

We can help children to become such biblically literate adults by working on these three catechetical goals:

A. Our ministry with children should help them to become knowledgeable and comfortable in using the Bible.

B. Our ministry with children should help them to know and understand the biblical story of salvation history.

C. Our ministry with children should help them to understand how to interpret Bible books and passages in their proper contexts.

Goal A is the **A**ccess goal. Goal B is the **Big Picture** goal. Goal C is the **C**ontext goal. Taken together, these can be called the ABCs of biblical literacy.

# The ABCs of Biblical Literacy

The three goals of biblical literacy follow a certain progression. The **Access** goal is the most basic goal; its competencies create a foundation for working on the **Big Picture** and **Context** goals. The **Big Picture** builds on the **Access** competencies and creates greater knowledge that the **Context** competencies can build on. All three goals are closely related; working on any one goal usually reinforces the others.

As a general guideline, with elementary-age children, your primary focus should be on the **Access** competencies and introducing some **Big Picture** knowledge. You will probably not focus on the **Context** competencies because they require more abstract reasoning than most young children are capable of. However, you will use specific **Context** skills and knowledge competencies as you teach children about the meaning of specific Bible stories.

Let's take a closer look at these three goals and how you can help children to develop the competencies needed to become proficient in them. (For a more detailed look at these three goals, read *Biblical Literacy Made Easy: A Practical Guide for Catechists, Teachers, and Youth Ministers*, Saint Mary's Press, 2008.)

## Implementing the Access Goal: Helping Children to Become Comfortable Using the Bible

Many children do not know how to use the Bible. They may have heard Bible stories, and maybe they were even given a Bible for their First Communion. But they do not know how the Bible is structured or how to find specific passages or stories within it. By focusing on the competencies of the **Access** goal, we can help the children we teach to become more familiar and comfortable with the Bible.

The most critical practice for achieving the **Access** goal—a practice so basic that many people overlook it—is simply having the children *use* the Bible. Too often children read Scripture passages as quotations in their textbooks. There may be only one Bible in the classroom, so the catechist looks up the passage and then hands the opened Bible to a young person to read. These practices do not encourage children to learn basic biblical literacy skills. If young Catholics are to become comfortable in accessing the Bible, they must use it regularly in our programs. Every classroom or meeting space must have enough Bibles for each student to use. When a Scripture story is referred to in a textbook, we can then have all the children look it up and read it from the Bible. What we model as important has a much greater impact than what we say is important!

To help children become comfortable in using the Bible, we can teach them two important competencies.

**Knowing the Bible's Structure** The Bible is not one book; rather it is a collection, or even a small library, of books and letters. These books are organized in a specific and intentional structure, sort of like books might be grouped in sections on a bookshelf. At the beginning of *The Catholic Children's Bible*, these sections are briefly explained and visually presented in the section called "The Bible Is Like a Bookshelf." Here is a slightly more detailed explanation of those sections:

- **The Old Testament** is the first major section of the Bible. Its books are primarily about God's relationship with his Chosen People, the Israelites (or the Jews).
  - The first part of the Old Testament is called the **Pentateuch**. The stories in these books are the heart of the Old Testament.
  - The second part of the Old Testament is called the **Historical Books**. These books recount how the Chosen People settled in the Promised Land and how they eventually became a kingdom ruled by great and not-so-great kings.
  - The third part of the Old Testament is called the **Wisdom Books**. These books teach some of the collected wisdom of the Israelites.
  - The fourth part of the Old Testament is called the **Books of the Prophets**. These contain the warnings and consolations of some of Israel's prophets.

- **The New Testament** is the second major section of the Bible. Its books tell how God fulfilled the Old Testament promises by sending us the Savior, Jesus Christ.
  - The first part of the New Testament is the four **Gospels and the Acts of the Apostles**. The Gospels have the stories about Christ's life and teaching, and the Book of Acts tells us about how the Church spread after Christ's Ascension.
  - The second part of the New Testament is the Letters. Early Church leaders sent these letters, some to specific individuals and others to specific Christian communities.
  - The last book of the New Testament is the **Book of Revelation**. It is a unique collection of prophecies and symbolic visions.

Refer to these sections when the children look up passages in the Bible. Say things like, "This Bible story is from the Book of Exodus, which is in the Old Testament of the Bible," or "This Bible story is from the Gospel of Mark. The Gospels have stories about the life of Jesus and the things he taught."

**Locating a Passage in the Bible** The system for finding a particular passage in the Bible is simple and explained in the beginning of *The Catholic Children's Bible* in the section called "How to Find a Bible Passage." After explaining this system to the children, help them to develop the skill of locating Bible passages through practice, practice, practice! This skill will take time for children to master, but it is a crucial skill for lifelong Bible reading. You will find help in teaching navigation skills to children, including practice exercises, in chapter 5 of this guide, "Helping Children to Navigate the Saint Mary's Press® *Catholic Children's Bible*."

## Implementing the Big Picture Goal: Helping Children to Know and Understand the Biblical Story of Salvation History

Because of our lectionary-based liturgies, Catholics are often familiar with most of the important people and stories of history. But if liturgies are a person's only contact with Scripture, she or he may not see how those individual stories fit into the overarching biblical story of God's covenantal relationship with the human race, which we also call salvation history. Much of Catholic theology is based on the presumption that we know and understand the overarching story of salvation history.

Salvation history is often organized into different periods to help us understand God's saving work. In all Saint Mary's Press resources eight historical periods are named to describe the arc of salvation history: Primeval History (the figurative stories in the Book of Genesis), the Patriarchs (Abraham, Isaac, and Jacob), Egypt and the Exodus (Moses and the desert experience of Israel), Settling the Promised Land (Joshua and the Twelve Tribes of Israel), the Kingdoms of Judah and Israel (the time of the Prophets), Exile and Return (the Babylonian Captivity and restoration of the Temple), Life of Jesus Christ, and the Early Christian Church.

Understanding how each biblical book's story fits into this bigger history is the mark of a truly biblically literate person. This kind of knowledge grows with repetition and review. You can best help young children to develop this knowledge by exposing them to key people and events in Scripture. *The Catholic Children's Bible* helps you to do this by focusing on 125 key people and events in the Featured Stories on two-page spreads. Using these Featured Stories consistently with children will provide them an excellent foundation for knowing and understanding salvation history.

# Implementing the Context Goal: Helping Children to Understand How to Interpret Bible Books and Passages in Their Proper Contexts

The **Context** goal is more subtle and complex than the **Access** and **Big Picture** goals. Catechists would typically not work on the skills required to master this goal with young children. It requires a level of abstract thinking that they are not yet capable of. However, catechists need to understand this goal in order to teach children the correct interpretation of the biblical stories they read.

This excerpt from the Second Vatican Council document *Dei Verbum* describes how to correctly interpret the Bible:

> Seeing that, in sacred scripture, God speaks through human beings in human fashion, it follows that the interpreters of sacred scripture, if they are to ascertain what God has wished to communicate to us, should carefully search out the meaning which the sacred writers really had in mind, the meaning which God had thought well to manifest through the medium of their words. (12)

This quotation states that we must do two things when interpreting a Bible story or teaching. First, we must seek to understand what the original human author intended to communicate. The Church Fathers called this the "literal sense" of Scripture. Second, we must seek to understand what God is revealing through the story or passage. The Church Fathers called this the fuller sense or the "spiritual sense" of Scripture. Often the literal sense and the spiritual sense of a passage are closely related. But in some Scripture passages, God reveals, through the spiritual sense, a deeper and more universal truth than the human author originally understood or intended.

Paragraphs 109–119 of the *Catechism of the Catholic Church* further explain how to apply these principles. These paragraphs describe the contexts we must consider when interpreting any particular passage of the Bible, which is why we describe this as the **Context** goal.

- **Historical context** To understand the full importance or meaning of a certain event, we need to know the larger historical situation the event occurred within.

- **Cultural context** Sometimes the true meaning of certain actions or words makes sense only when we understand the cultural practices or beliefs of the time.

- **Literary genre** The Bible is composed of many different types of literature. We must know which type we are reading and realize that each genre has its own rules for interpretation.

- **Unity of the whole Bible** When taken as a whole, God's revealed truth is presented in the Bible without error. This is the case in many Old Testament passages, whose Christian meaning can be completely and accurately understood only in light of the New Testament revelation.

- **Living Tradition of the Church** To fully understand some Bible passages, we must take into account how the Magisterium—the official teaching authority of the Church—has interpreted the meaning of those passages.

- **Coherence of the truths of faith** When it comes to religious or moral truth, the Bible cannot contradict itself or any other revealed truth of our Tradition.

If we do not interpret the Bible using these contexts, we could easily misinterpret God's Revelation. This is the danger of biblical fundamentalism, an approach to biblical interpretation that Catholics are cautioned to avoid. In its extreme forms, biblical fundamentalism leads people to false beliefs, such as the belief that God created the universe in six twenty-four-hour days.

Even though you will not necessarily mention these different contexts when working with young children, the Featured Stories in *The Catholic Children's Bible* provide trustworthy tools to help children correctly understand the contexts of 125 Bible stories. The engaging art provides strong visual cues about the human author's intention. The Tell It! panels provide children the opportunity to retell the story using the visual prompts so that they begin to process its meaning. And the short Understand It! panels explain what God is revealing through the story, drawing upon the contexts of the unity of the Bible, Tradition, and the coherence of the truths of faith.

# The Dark Passages of Scripture

In helping children to read and understand the Bible, catechists and teachers must be aware that some Bible stories are not child-friendly. The accounts of incest, rape, genocide, and holy war in the sacred pages of Scripture can come as a surprise for many beginning Bible readers. In his apostolic exhortation *Verbum Domini (The Word of the Lord)*, published in November 2010, Pope Benedict XVI calls these stories the "dark" passages of the Bible. Here is what the Holy Father says regarding these passages:

> In discussing the relationship between the Old and the New Testaments, the Synod also considered those passages in the Bible which, due to the violence and immorality they occasionally contain, prove obscure and difficult. Here it must be remembered first and foremost that *biblical revelation is deeply rooted in history.* God's plan is manifested *progressively* and it is accomplished slowly, *in successive stages* and despite human resistance. God chose a people and patiently worked to guide and educate them. Revelation is suited to the cultural and moral level of distant times and thus describes facts and customs, such as cheating and trickery, and acts of violence and massacre, without explicitly denouncing the

immorality of such things. This can be explained by the historical context, yet it can cause the modern reader to be taken aback, especially if he or she fails to take account of the many "dark" deeds carried out down the centuries, and also in our own day. In the Old Testament, the preaching of the prophets vigorously challenged every kind of injustice and violence, whether collective or individual, and thus became God's way of training his people in preparation for the Gospel. So it would be a mistake to neglect those passages of Scripture that strike us as problematic. Rather, we should be aware that the correct interpretation of these passages requires a degree of expertise, acquired through a training that interprets the texts in their historical-literary context and within the Christian perspective which has as its ultimate hermeneutical key "the Gospel and the new commandment of Jesus Christ brought about in the paschal mystery."[1] I encourage scholars and pastors to help all the faithful to approach these passages through an interpretation which enables their meaning to emerge in the light of the mystery of Christ. (42)

In this teaching, Pope Benedict emphasizes the following points:

- The Bible does not shy away from telling about the worst things that humans do to one another—these are the very things that Jesus Christ came to save us from. Unfortunately, these evil acts continue even into our time.

- The biblical author does not always explicitly say that a particular action is immoral; at the time he was writing, these actions might not have yet been seen as immoral (such as the killing of whole groups of people) or because the biblical author presumed the reader knew that these were immoral actions (such as Lot's daughters having sexual relations with their drunken father). Because God's Revelation is "manifested *progressively*" and "is accomplished slowly, *in successive stages*," the preaching of the prophets and ultimately the teaching of Jesus Christ helps us to see the true moral meaning of these actions.

- To properly understand these passages requires the help of people trained in biblical interpretation, such as pastors and biblical scholars.

So what does this mean for you as a catechist or teacher of young children when it comes to these dark passages of Scripture? The best advice is to avoid these passages completely because these stories can be too disturbing and confusing for young and innocent minds. *The Catholic Children's Bible* does not use any of these stories in the Featured Stories, so you do not have to worry about coming across any dark stories when you use these special two-page spreads!

# Chapter 4

## Looking through the Saint Mary's Press® *Catholic Children's Bible*

The Saint Mary's Press *Catholic Children's Bible* is no ordinary Bible! Developed especially for children and those who are eager to introduce children to the treasures of Scripture, *The Catholic Children's Bible* provides many helps to the reader and teacher. These are listed in the table of contents, both before and after the main body of the Bible itself.

## At the Front of *The Catholic Children's Bible*

Let's take a look at the sections in the front of the Bible:

### Featured Stories

This is simply a list of the stories in *The Catholic Children's Bible* that are illustrated and surrounded by instructive features: Understand It!, Live It!, and Tell It! The Scripture reference is also given for each story so that you can easily find the particular story that you wish to present to the children.

### Welcome!

This section welcomes the reader to *The Catholic Children's Bible* and briefly explains the components of the Featured Story pages.

### How to Find a Bible Passage

This section presents a straightforward instruction on finding a particular passage in the Bible according to book, chapter, and verse. Further strategies, including three handouts, to help children find passages in *The Catholic Children's Bible,* are presented in chapter 5, "Helping Children to Navigate the Saint Mary's Press®*Catholic Children's Bible.*"

## The Bible Is Like a Bookshelf

This section presents the books of the Bible as a bookshelf containing seventy-three books. This illustration will prove helpful when explaining the division of the Bible into two sections, the Old Testament and the New Testament. In addition, *The Catholic Children's Bible* is color coded: the color at the bottom of the page is the same color as a particular section of the Bible (the Pentateuch, the Historical Books, etc.). The next chapter in this guide, "Helping Children to Navigate the Saint Mary's Press® *Catholic Children's Bible,*" offers strategies for presenting the organization of the Bible to the children.

## Pronunciation Key

This section outlines a phonetic pronunciation key as an aid to pronouncing the often unfamiliar names of people and places found in the Bible.

# At the Back of *The Catholic Children's Bible*

In the flurry of preparation, sometimes the information found at the back of a book can be neglected. Be sure to look at the back of *The Catholic Children's Bible*! You will find the following helpful sections there:

Bible Pictures . . . . . . . . . . . . . . . . . . . . . . . . . . . . . . . . . . . . . . . 1978
Bible Time Line . . . . . . . . . . . . . . . . . . . . . . . . . . . . . . . . . . . . . . 1984
Bible Maps . . . . . . . . . . . . . . . . . . . . . . . . . . . . . . . . . . . . . . . . . 1986
Catholic Practices . . . . . . . . . . . . . . . . . . . . . . . . . . . . . . . . . . . . 1990
Catholic Prayers . . . . . . . . . . . . . . . . . . . . . . . . . . . . . . . . . . . . . 1992
Bible Passages for Special Times . . . . . . . . . . . . . . . . . . . . . . . . . 2000

When preparing a lesson on a particular story or passage, look to see if any of these "back of the book" resources can be helpful to you.

# The Books of the Bible

This brings us to the main section of *The Catholic Children's Bible:* the Bible itself. You will see that each part of the Bible, the Old Testament and the New Testament, has an introduction. Then the books of the Bible are listed in six distinct parts and are clearly marked: the Pentateuch, the Historical Books, the Wisdom Books, the Books of the Prophets, the Gospels and the Acts of the Apostles, the Letters and Revelation.

Such a big book, with so many parts, can be overwhelming to both teachers and children. The next chapter, "Helping Children to Navigate the Saint Mary's Press® *Catholic Children's Bible,*" not only suggests strategies to help children find Scripture passages but also explains the color coding of *The Catholic Children's Bible* and provides handouts for practice exercises. This will help the children become familiar with *The Catholic Children's Bible* in an organized way. These simple exercises will help you to "clear a path" (see Isaiah 40:3 and Matthew 3:3) for the Word of the Lord to enter into the lives of your young Bible students.

# Chapter 5

## Helping Children to Navigate the Saint Mary's Press® *Catholic Children's Bible*

### Introducing the Bible to Children

As noted in the "Welcome" to *The Catholic Children's Bible*, this is a BIG book! Introducing it to children is best done in three ways: (1) explaining that the Bible is the Word of God, and perhaps having a Bible enthronement ceremony to emphasize the sacredness of God's Word; (2) using a "hands-on approach" to explain and explore the color coding of *The Catholic Children's Bible;* and (3) using the handouts included with this chapter as practice exercises in navigating *The Catholic Children's Bible.*

### The Bible Is the Word of God

This is the primary message to communicate when teaching children about the Bible. The Bible was written by people who listened to God and were inspired by the Holy Spirit to write down the important truths we need to know to follow God's way, to know and love his Son Jesus, and to love one another. In the Bible, God speaks to us in many different ways—through stories and poems, and even, in the Book of Psalms, songs that were sung by the people. We still sing these songs today at the Eucharist.

As actions speak louder than words, you may want to have a short Bible enthronement at the beginning of a class session. An outline for such an enthronement can be found in chapter 7 of this guide ("Teaching Scripture to Children"), on page 33, "Shaping Attitudes toward the Bible."

## Exploring *The Catholic Children's Bible,* Live and In Color

### Bottom Bands of Color

When you open *The Catholic Children's Bible,* you will notice bands of color along the bottoms of the pages. These bands of color are *not* for decorative use only! They delineate the major divisions of the Bible as follows:

| Section of the Bible | Books of the Bible | Color of Bottom Band |
|---|---|---|
| | (see Bible Table of Contents) | |
| The Pentateuch (or Torah) | Genesis through Deuteronomy | aqua |
| The Historical Books | Joshua through 2 Maccabees | brown |
| The Wisdom Books | Job through Sirach | purple |
| The Books of the Prophets | Isaiah through Malachi | orange |
| The Gospels and the Acts of the Apostles | Matthew, Mark, Luke, John, and the Acts of the Apostles | blue |
| The Letters and Revelation | Romans through Revelation | green |
| Prayer and Bible helps | back of the book | yellow |

## Colored Tabs

You will also notice that *The Catholic Children's Bible* is tabbed along the sides. Each book of the Bible has its own distinctive color, matching the title of the particular book on the first page of the book, and each tab is labeled with the name of the book. This makes it very easy for children to find a particular book. You will also notice that the chapter number is included in the tab. On the left-hand tab, the chapter number notes the chapter at the top of the page. On the right-hand tab, the chapter number notes the chapter at the bottom of that page.

## Featured Stories Stand Out

Perhaps the most attractive elements of *The Catholic Children's Bible* are the Featured Stories. These stories encapsulate a Scripture story or passage, illustrate it, and surround it with the helpful Understand It!, Live It!, and Tell It! teaching aids. In addition, new or unfamiliar words are printed in bold type and listed, with definitions, on the first page of each Featured Story.

While reading through the text of the Bible and a particular book, you will notice a green leaf and a swash of color running across a column. This alerts you to the beginning of the "full story" of the Featured Story. The citation for this "full story" is printed in small type on the first page of the Featured Story, above the Scripture verses. Another green leaf and a swash of color alerts you to the end of the full story. For example, on the first page of the Featured Story "God Made Us to Love and to Be Loved," we find in small type: "For the full story, read Genesis 2:5–25." If you look up Genesis, chapter 2, you will find a green leaf and a swash of color at verse 5, and another green leaf and swash of color at verse 25.

## Finding Specific Passages in *The Catholic Children's Bible*

As you will note in the table of contents of *The Catholic Children's Bible*, there is an article titled "How to Find a Bible Passage." This short article presents the traditional method of finding specific Bible passages by the name of the book, the chapter, and the verse. This is basic information for anyone of any age who wishes to locate a particular Bible passage.

*The Catholic Children's Bible*, however, introduces the use of color to enable children to find Scripture passages more easily. The next few pages emphasize finding the books of the Bible, outlining some child-friendly group exercises for finding Scripture passages, broken down into easy steps. Only after that skill is mastered do children learn to find a chapter and a verse in a particular book.

## Group Exercise 1: Finding Book, Chapter, and Verse

Objective: To help children find the various books of the Bible and identify them by color. The exercise can be extended into finding chapters and verses of particular books.

1. Explain that we will begin exploring the Bible by finding various books.
   > I will say the name of the book, and I will also write it on the board. When you find it, raise your hand quietly. Don't shout out the name! When everyone's hand is raised, I will ask: What color is (name of book)? And then all of you will say together the color of the book. Let's begin.
   > Find the Book of Genesis. All hands up? What color is the Book of Genesis?
   **All respond:** Yellow!
   > Find the Book of Numbers. All hands up? What color is the Book of Numbers?
   **All respond:** Orange!

2. Continue in this way, using both the Old and the New Testaments, until you are confident that the children can find the books of the Bible.

3. After the children have mastered finding books, continue in this way, asking them to find first a book and then a particular chapter of that book. Once the children have found various chapters, ask them to find particular verses. Then choose a book

and write a Scripture reference from it on the board (for example, Exodus 20:8). Explain each part of this citation, and ask the children to find it in their Bibles.

## Group Exercise 2: Identifying the Categories of Bible Books

In an introductory article to *The Catholic Children's Bible*, "The Bible Is Like a Bookshelf," the reader is introduced to the bands of color at the bottom of the pages of the Bible. Each color represents a category of scriptural writing. You can introduce these categories to the children in this way:

1. Ask the children to turn to the illustration of the Bible bookshelf on page 15 in *The Catholic Children's Bible*. Then share the following:
   > I will name one book of the Bible. When you find it and point to it, raise your hand. Then, when all hands are raised, I will ask the color of the whole section where that book is found on the bookshelf. This is the color of the kind of book that this particular book is. Let's try it.
   > Find the Book of Exodus on the bookshelf. All hands up? What color is the whole section where you found the Book of Exodus? *(aqua)* This means that the Book of Exodus belongs to the Pentateuch, the first five books of the Bible.
   > Now find the Book of Exodus in your Bible. What color is the band at the bottom? *(aqua)* This color reminds you that the Book of Exodus belongs to the Pentateuch. All the books with this color on the bottom belong to the Pentateuch.
   > Find the Book of Ruth in the bookshelf. All hands up? What color is the whole section where you found the Book of Ruth? *(brown)* This means that the Book of Ruth belongs to the Historical Books.
   > Now find the Book of Ruth in your Bible. What color is the band at the bottom? *(brown)* This color reminds you that the Book of Ruth belongs to the Historical Books of the Bible. All the books with this color on the bottom belong to the Historical Books.

2. Continue in this way, asking the children to find one book in each of the categories of biblical books, always reminding them to look at the band of color on the bottom to identify the particular category to which a book belongs.

## Bible Search Challenges (Handouts)

At the end of this chapter are three Bible search challenges. These are handouts of graduated difficulty. The first, "Bible Search Challenge 1," is the easiest; the last, "Bible Search Challenge 3," is the most difficult (categories of biblical books are searched in this challenge only). Older children will be able to work out these challenges one after the other. Present them to younger children in stages, as the children grow in proficiency at finding Scripture verses. You might like to have the students form pairs to complete the Bible search challenges. The answers are given in the following section.

## Answers to Bible Search Challenges

### Challenge 1

*Matching:* Column I: 1, 4, 7, 8, 7, 3, 5. Column II: 8, 1, 3, 7, 1, 1.
*Sentence completion:* lights; Lord; people; salt; riches, people, soon.

### Challenge 2

*Matching:* 6, 5, 7, 8, 2, 4, 1, 3.
*A Bible prayer:* Lord, teach us to follow your way, each and every day!

### Challenge 3

Amos (Prophets, orange)
1 Corinthians (Letters, green)
Deuteronomy (the Pentateuch, aqua)
Hebrews (Letters, green)
Jeremiah (Prophets, orange)
John (Gospels, blue)
1 Kings (Historical Books, brown)
Leviticus (the Pentateuch, aqua)
Mark (the Gospels, blue)
Proverbs (Wisdom Books, purple)
Sirach (Wisdom Books, purple)
Tobit (Historical Books, brown)

# Bible Search Challenge 1

1. Match each book of the Bible with the color of its tab by writing the number of the color on the line next to the name of the book: (1) yellow, (2) green, (3) blue, (4) orange, (5) purple, (6) light brown, (7) aqua, (8) pink

\_\_\_\_\_ Genesis               \_\_\_\_\_ Micah

\_\_\_\_\_ Numbers               \_\_\_\_\_ Luke

\_\_\_\_\_ Judges                \_\_\_\_\_ Acts of the Apostles

\_\_\_\_\_ Ruth                  \_\_\_\_\_ Galatians

\_\_\_\_\_ Psalms                \_\_\_\_\_ Hebrews

\_\_\_\_\_ Wisdom                \_\_\_\_\_ Revelation

\_\_\_\_\_ Isaiah

2. Complete the following sentences by finding the missing word in each Scripture verse:

Genesis 1:17: "He placed the _____ in the sky to shine on the earth."

Psalm 23:1: "The _____ is my shepherd."

Isaiah 9:2: "The _____ who walked in darkness / have seen a great light."

Matthew 5:13: "You are like _____ for the whole human race."

Romans 11:33: "How great are God's _____!"

Titus 3:14: "Our _____ must learn to spend their time doing good."

Revelation 22:7: "'Listen!' says Jesus. 'I am coming _____.'"

# Bible Search Challenge 2

1.  Match the words with the verses below. Find the verse in column 1, and then match it to one of the words in that verse found in column 2.

| **Column 1** | **Column 2** |
|---|---|
| _____ Exodus 33:14 | 1. Spirit |
| _____ 1 Samuel 17:20 | 2. justice |
| _____ Ezra 7:27 | 3. loved |
| _____ Psalm 136 | 4. servant |
| _____ Wisdom 1:1 | 5. morning |
| _____ Isaiah 49:5 | 6. victory |
| _____ Joel 2:28 | 7. Praise |
| _____ Malachi 1:2 | 8. good |

2.  Each of the verses below contains a certain word (first word, second word, third word, and so on). Find the word and write it in the blank. When you finish, you will have a new prayer made up of words you have found in the Bible!

Psalm 135:1 (third word) _____

Matthew 13:1 (last word) _____

1 Samuel 4:8 (fourth word) _____

Exodus 32:8 (eleventh and twelfth words) _____ _____,

Psalm 17:5 (sixth and seventh words) _____ _____,

Genesis 7:15 (seventh word) _____ and

Psalm 139:5 (seventh word) _____

Psalm 139:5 (seventh word) _____

Genesis 1:23 (tenth word) _____!

Document #: TX003046

# Bible Search Challenge 3

1. For each book of the Bible below, write its category and its bottom color band as found in *The Catholic Children's Bible*. But first see if you can identify the category of the book without looking at your Bible. Then check *The Catholic Children's Bible* for the correct category and color band.

   **Categories:** The Pentateuch, Historical Books, Wisdom Books, Prophets, Gospels and the Acts of the Apostles, Letters and Revelation

| Book of the Bible | Category | Color Band |
|---|---|---|
| Amos | | |
| 1 Corinthians | | |
| Deuteronomy | | |
| Hebrews | | |
| Jeremiah | | |
| John | | |
| 1 Kings | | |
| Leviticus | | |
| Mark | | |
| Proverbs | | |
| Sirach | | |
| Tobit | | |

2. Take this mind-bending challenge! Memorize the books of the Bible, category by category. Start with the Pentateuch and the Gospels and Acts of the Apostles, then move on to the other categories. You will amaze your teachers and astound your friends!

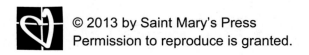

# Chapter 6

## Characteristics of Second, Third, and Fourth Graders

Although all children are distinct individuals with different rates of development, children of the same age do have some common developmental elements. Thus, in this section, we discuss some characteristics of each age group. A better understanding of the various ages will help you to be more effective in spreading the Good News.

One characteristic common of second, third, and fourth graders is high energy! Children of this age are active and curious learners who will ask and say the most surprising things. And, though they share the common characteristics we outline in this chapter, we can never forget that each one of them is unique, with his or her own individual characteristics and gifts.

## Second Graders

Second graders are lively, yet more grown-up and serious compared to the less confident first graders they were just a year ago. Now that second graders have a few years of elementary school experience, they are more settled and comfortable in their learning environment. The seven- to eight-year-old typically appreciates the facts, order, and structure of a classroom or catechetical setting. Thus, being organized and well-prepared will help your second graders to feel relaxed, content, and ready to learn.

### Physical Characteristics

Most second graders have good hand-eye coordination and therefore are fairly adept at writing, painting, drawing, cutting, and pasting. Because they are still growing rapidly, they may be somewhat awkward at some of these tasks. However, in general they have good large- and small-muscle motor skills.

### Intellectual Characteristics

Second graders are concrete thinkers, but they do have some analytical skills and can organize their thoughts. For example, they can make comparisons and think reflectively. Yet, most of their thinking is concrete and focuses on the physical things that they can see or imagine. They might have trouble imagining something with which they are unfamiliar (see *Grade-by-Grade Learning*, at pbs.org). For example, they may have trouble imagining a desert if they have never seen one. So, if knowing what a desert is like is an important part of a lesson, you may need to show them a picture or a video clip of a desert.

Furthermore, second graders do have the ability to distinguish between right and wrong, although they will not always understand the consequences of their actions. They do, however, like to please adults.

### Social-Emotional Characteristics

The second-grade child is developing a sense of self. Interaction with classmates helps the child, but there are times when a second grader may want to be alone. And, friendships can change quickly in second grade. At the same time, the seven- to eight-year-old child likes to play and work with friends. For this reason, second graders do best working with a partner or in a small group. Also, this is the period when the division of sexes begins, meaning that children prefer to play or work with others of the same sex. Given that there is a heightened interest in friendships at this age, it is a good time to talk about Jesus as friend.

## Third Graders

Third graders are spirited, lively, and eager to take on more challenging, complicated tasks. However, they do not necessarily have all the follow-through skills needed to complete their tasks. Although they will take some initiative and work enthusiastically, you will have to help them to stay organized.

### Physical Characteristics

Coordination and balance are much improved for third-grade children. Their muscle groups and their fine motor skills have developed to the point that they can do more intricate tasks beyond writing and drawing. They have the ability to use small instruments and thus can do things like simple sewing or threading small beads onto a string.

### Intellectual Characteristics

Verbal skills are in high gear by third grade. Most third graders have mastered a grade-level ability for reading, writing, and listening. They also like to talk and discuss their ideas. They are inquisitive, and now they want to know not just the facts but also the reasons behind the facts. For example, third graders may want to know why Jesus was born in a stable in Bethlehem, or why he asked James and John to leave their father to be his disciples. And, they are ready and willing to discuss the importance of these facts.

This deeper level of thinking helps them to evaluate and make judgments. They are beginning to see the connections between concepts, and they are beginning to think abstractly. They not only know the difference between right and wrong but can also usually understand the consequences of various choices they make.

### Social-Emotional Characteristics

In third grade, the peer group is very important, and peer pressure can become an issue. Also, it is fairly common to have a "best friend," though sometimes to the exclusion of other children. You can build on the notion of Jesus as friend and use examples of Jesus and how he treated his friends. Point out that Jesus welcomed many friends, like Peter and the Apostles, Martha, Mary, Zacchaeus, and others.

Playing in same-sex groups is also still the norm. Most third graders enjoy the social dimension of working in groups and having group discussions. They can also work effectively in small groups to complete a simple task.

## Fourth Graders

Fourth graders are now some of the older children in their elementary school. Thus, they often feel pretty mature, important, and more autonomous. They are willing to work independently and have less need for adult direction. They are ready to take on more responsibility and make decisions. Indeed, this is a good age to discuss the responsibilities of discipleship. Fourth graders may also develop particular interests in a hobby, sport, or activity, and they may take it very seriously.

### Physical Characteristics

Girls are more physically mature than boys at this point. Some girls have begun pre-puberty and even puberty. Girls and boys alike may be more temperamental and brooding. But, at the same time, they are still high energy and still like to play outside and play with friends. They may also like to play team sports.

### Intellectual Characteristics

Fourth graders are able to do some abstract thinking and reasoning, but they still do best with concrete, hands-on learning. They like using books and references, and they have an interest in facts and figures. They also have a developing conscience and definitely have a sense of what is fair, right, and just. These interests make it a good time to have them delve more deeply into the Scripture stories that have moral lessons, as most of them do. For instance, a fourth grader will be intrigued by the fact that Jesus tells Peter he should forgive not seven times but seventy times seven times. Why would Jesus ask us to keep forgiving someone who keeps sinning?

Also, nine- to ten-year-olds have the capacity to complete a more complicated and prolonged project. So, for example, with guidance from you, a small group can take a Scripture story and act it out as a skit.

## Social-Emotional Characteristics

This is an age for high emotions and dramatic intensity, especially among girls. Fourth graders are often critical of themselves and others and sometimes express this inappropriately by talking about friends and classmates. Many fourth graders are interested in the opposite sex. Even when this is the case, however, most still want to stay within their same-sex groups for socializing. In addition, they like working in small groups and can even come to a group decision. Again, emphasizing that Jesus wants us not only to welcome one another as friends but also to love and help one another can lead fourth graders to develop empathy and respect for those they may not naturally like.

## Summary

In each age-group, we have presented very general characteristics. Although these characteristics might not describe every child, an awareness of these qualities will help you to plan developmentally appropriate learning activities for your group. The more you learn about the spectrum of child development, the more you will understand where the children you teach have "come from" and where they are headed in their next phase of development. Each child develops at his or her own pace, and it is likely an uneven pace at that! One child may be far ahead intellectually but a little behind in social development. Another child's social development may be right on target, but he or she may face challenges in thinking skills. The activities in this guide are so varied that you are sure to find some to meet almost every child's need to grow intellectually, emotionally, and spiritually.

One way to give every child a chance to grow and develop in your classroom, even if a group meets only once a week, is to give each child a job. Line leader, paper passer, prayer leader, movement leader, Bible carrier—whatever small job is available should be assigned for one session (or one week), and then reassigned for the next one. Keep a running list of assignments so that each child gets a turn at doing each job. Write the assignments for each session on the board. Elementary-age children love to help and to feel appreciated, and you will be rewarded with a smooth-running group of proud and happy children.

# Chapter 7

## Teaching Scripture to Children

According to the Gospels, Jesus clearly wants children to come to him. We can fulfill his desire by leading them to Scripture. Jesus, the Word, is present in the words of Sacred Scripture. Through them he speaks to children's hearts just as he speaks to ours. There are ways to facilitate this encounter for his young disciples.

### Creating a Christian Environment

As you begin Bible study, impress on the children the holiness of what you are doing. Explain that you and they are the Church in miniature. You are gathered to hear the Good News about Jesus that Scripture contains, to think about what he is saying to you, and to grow in your friendship with him. Remind the children of these facts periodically.

The room where you meet is holy space. As such, it should be neat, attractive, quiet, and free from distractions. Religious pictures and statues help to set the tone, and a Christian song playing softly before the session helps the children to focus on God. Praying before and after the sessions sends the message that this is special time.

### Creating a Loving Atmosphere

Christians are one with Jesus and one another. Our classrooms should be characterized by love, the hallmark of Christians. As teachers, our bearing, our tone of voice, the way we move, and even how we dress convey our love for Jesus and the children as much as the words we speak. As soon as possible, learn the children's names and something about each child. Play ice-breaker games to help the children get to know one another. Be quick to praise the children as a whole class and individually. Point out the gifts of each child and show appreciation for them.

### Create a Loving and Respectful Community

To build a loving and respectful community, plan opportunities for each child to contribute to the class. Sometimes arrange for the children to work together on projects. Make kindness a classroom rule, and encourage the children to help one another. Above all, treat the children equally, fairly, and with respect. When the children know you care about them, and when they care about one another, they are less likely to misbehave. They will not want to disappoint you! To forestall discipline problems, prepare lessons that keep the children active and engaged. (If you sense restlessness in the group, interrupt your lesson by having the children listen to or sing a scriptural song. You may want to add movements and ask the group to follow you in prayerful song and dance.) If a child does disrupt the class, speak to him or her privately. If necessary, enlist the aid of the parents.

## Shaping Attitudes toward the Bible

Teach the children that the Bible is the Word of God. Because God is its author, the Bible is holy. It should not be placed on the floor. To instill awe for the Bible, create a Bible corner by keeping a large, beautiful Bible on a table or shelf covered with a lovely cloth. Set a candle near it (if fire laws allow) and sometimes light it when the Bible is read. Add, or let the children add, flowers, a plant, or colored leaves to the display. When reading from the Bible, hold it reverently, turn pages carefully, and use a dignified voice.

At least once hold a prayer service honoring the Bible. Sing a song about God's Word, read verses about it (see Psalm 119, Matthew 7:24–29, Matthew 13:1–9, Hebrews 4:12), and process with the Bible held high. Conclude by setting the Bible in its special place and having everyone bow to it one by one. You might burn incense near the Bible.

## Preparing to Teach a Bible Story

Read a Bible commentary beforehand to get insights into the story. This will also enable you to answer children's questions more knowledgeably. Prepare the children for a Bible story by defining unfamiliar words and explaining new concepts. Then invoke the Holy Spirit in a brief prayer such as, "Holy Spirit, open our ears, our minds, and our hearts to receive the message you have for us today."

Variety is the spice of life. It also prevents boring lessons. You can read the story to the class or call on children to read it, but occasionally try these methods:

1. Ask a question or make a comment that leads into the story. Then have the children read the story independently and discuss it.

2. Record a dramatic reading. Change your voice for different characters. Add sound effects. When you play the recording, invite the children to close their eyes.

3. If the story has speaking parts, appoint a narrator and children to read the parts.

4. Have each child in the class read one sentence or verse.

5. Call on a child to read a few sentences and then to choose a classmate to continue. Continue in this way throughout the entire story.

6. Have the class read the story in unison.

7. Write the story's verses on slips of paper and number them. Put them in a bag or box and let the children choose one. Arrange the children in order and have them read their verses in turn.

## Telling a Bible Story

You may wish to tell a Bible story before the children read it or for review. Check the list below for a few storytelling techniques that will delight the class and make the story more memorable.

### What You Can Do to Tell the Story

1. Use gestures, movement, and expression. Vary the speed and volume of your voice. You might even dress like a character.

2. Ask questions as you tell the story to maintain interest and stimulate thinking. But keep them simple so they do not distract.

3. Add sensory words to bring the story to life. Let the children see, hear, smell, taste, and feel the story as if they were there.

4. Make comments that link the story to the children's world. Refer to current news, famous people, and what the children know and experience.

5. Use flannel board figures, dolls, stuffed animals, puppets, or pipe cleaner figures.

6. Do a chalk talk, preferably with colored chalk—even if you aren't a good artist.

7. Tear or fold paper to form a shape as you talk—for example, a whale for Jonah, a star for the Nativity, and a lily for the Resurrection. Craft books can provide ideas for these models.

8. Tell the story by interviewing someone posing as a person in the story or a as a witness to it.

9. Think of colors that match parts of the story. Show construction paper of those colors at the appropriate times.

10. Post or project a picture of the story. Or reveal several of them as you tell the story. These might be glued to the sides of a box.

### *What the Children Can Do as the Story Is Told*

1. Distribute pictures of people and objects from the story. When the person or object is mentioned, the child holding it stands and raises it high or posts it to a sheet of newsprint.

2. Have the children to draw on paper or work with clay as the Spirit moves them.

3. Direct the children to respond with a word or action when they hear a certain word. For example, in the story of the Fall, they could hiss at the word *snake*.

4. Do an action as your read each sentence, and have the children repeat the sentence and the action.

## Reinforcing the Bible Stories

Children are usually eager to tell and retell familiar stories. In their spontaneous play, they "act out" stories they see on television and roles they experience in their families. Acting out Bible stories, as well as learning related poems and songs, are ways children can use their natural gifts of role-play, music, and rhyme.

### *Plays*

Help the children to act out the story using symbols, identifying headbands or signs, costumes, props, scenery drawn on the board, and sound effects. The book *Gospel Theatre for the Whole Community* (Twenty-Third Publications, 2006) provides simple scripts for all the Gospel stories. The children can present the play to another class or their families.

*The Greatest Adventure: Stories from the Bible* (Hanna-Barbera, 1985–1993) presents animated Bible stories on DVD and VHS. These are available through online booksellers.

### *Songs and Movement*

Teach Scripture-related songs. Some hymns sung in church are based on Scripture. Bible songs geared to children can be found in collections like the hymnal *Rise Up and Sing* and the CDs *Stories and Songs of Jesus* and *More Stories and Songs of Jesus* (all from Oregon Catholic Press). The book and CD *Wee Sing Bible Songs* (Price Stern Sloan) contains well-loved children's songs. As appropriate, invite the children to follow your example as you move prayerfully to these songs, or lead the children around the room in a march, procession, or dance. If singing is "praying twice," as Saint Augustine says, perhaps those who move and dance as they sing are praying three times!

*Poems*

A favorite of teachers and children for decades is the Arch Book series (Concordia Publishing House). Each book tells a Bible story in rhyme.

## Memorizing God's Word

In Psalm 119:11 we pray, "I keep your law in my heart." By memorizing Scripture verses, the children create a storehouse of God's words to draw on for guidance and for prayer. It is important that the children understand the verses before committing them to memory. Here are three ideas for helping children to memorize Scripture verses:

1. Write a verse on the board. Erase one word or phrase and have the children recite the verse. Continue until all the words are erased.

2. Create a jigsaw puzzle with words from the verse on each piece. Time the children as they assemble the puzzle, and challenge them to beat their time. You might make several sets and let groups race to assemble them.

3. Have the students toss a soft item to one another. Each child who receives the item must recite a chosen verse or add a word to it.

## A Legacy of Love for Scripture

The key factor in teaching children Scripture is your own love for it. When you treasure God's Word, it will show, and the children will catch your attitude. Then the time spent reading and studying the Bible will be a joy for you and the children. You will be handing on a legacy of love for Scripture that will stay with the children for the rest of their lives.

# Chapter 8

## Scriptural Prayer with Children

### Strategies

Among the many ways to pray, scriptural prayer is one of the best for children. The stories, images, characters, and words of the Bible are an excellent point of departure for a child's prayer. What better way to begin praying than to start with God's own Word? Using Scripture as a foundation for prayer helps children to engage their imagination and in turn, express their hopes, thoughts, and concerns.

Before we turn to the various methods used when we pray with Scripture, let's consider a few general recommendations for praying with children.

### Tip 1: Teach Children to Pray

Although some children are very comfortable with prayer, many children are not experienced with prayer and therefore need to be taught to pray. Don't assume that all children know how to pray or even know what prayer is. When you first start praying with the children, explain that praying is talking and listening to God.

#### Talking to God

When we "talk" to God in prayer, we can use words spoken aloud or words spoken silently in our hearts or words written on paper. We can talk to God through song or drawing or works of art. We can also talk to God by using God's gift of imagination.

#### Listening to God

When we "listen" to God in prayer, we do not usually hear spoken words; rather, God communicates to us in a variety of ways. When we pray, sometimes the ideas, thoughts, and feelings we have are from God. Furthermore, when we use scriptural prayer, we hear God's own Word.

In scriptural prayer, we listen to God's voice by doing the following:

- Listening to the readings from the Bible (Did something in the reading catch my attention? Did God or Jesus or one of the other characters seem to be talking *to me?*)

- Being aware of thoughts and ideas that come to mind when we think about the Scripture readings (Did the Scripture story give me an idea or make me think about a particular person or situation in my life?)

- Being aware of our feelings and emotions (Did the reading make me feel warm and cozy? Did it make me uncomfortable or curious? What do the feelings tell me?)

## Tip 2: Keep It Simple

The best way to teach prayer to children is to model it. Keep explanations to a minimum and simply model various methods of scriptural prayer. We want children to know that we can pray anywhere and anytime. Prayer does not need to be a complicated production. Let it come from your heart.

## Tip 3: Teach Various Forms of Prayer

Many children will be familiar with prayer in which we ask God for something or we ask God for help. Children are very good at asking God to heal a sick grandparent or to help them on a test. Lead children to understand that there are many other forms of prayer:

- Prayers of petition: We ask God for what we need or want.

- Prayers of thanksgiving: We thank God for all that we have.

- Prayers of praise: We give glory to God for all that he is.

- Prayers of contrition: We express sorrow for our sin.

All these forms of prayer can be scriptural prayer. Children can give God thanks and praise using scriptural prayer. Or, they can make a special request of God using the words of Scripture.

# Ways to Pray Scripture with Children

## Vocal Prayer

One of the first, most comfortable ways of praying is to pray a familiar prayer aloud with the children. Of course, the Lord's Prayer is one of our most beloved scriptural prayers (see Matthew 6:9–13). In addition, *The Catholic Children's Bible* provides other written prayers that children can pray together. For example, in Luke 12:22–24, Jesus tells us not to worry. Then, in the Live It! panel following the story, is a written prayer that children can read and pray aloud together. Throughout *The Catholic Children's Bible*, particularly in the Live It! panels, both traditional prayers (like the prayer to a guardian angel found in the Featured Story "Adam and Eve Disobey God" in the Book of Genesis) and prayers rooted in Scripture are provided for children to pray, alone or with others.

## Spontaneous Prayer

Another type of vocal prayer is spontaneous prayer. In spontaneous prayer, the children are free to choose their own words when addressing God. Typically, after discussing or reflecting on a particular Scripture story, children are invited to pray freely using the given Scripture story or passage as their inspiration. Often it is helpful to give children a simple prompt or a few words to help them get started.

For example, in Acts 1:3–11 (Featured Story "Jesus Is Taken into Heaven"), the children hear about the Apostles' being filled with the power of the Holy Spirit. Afterward, in the Live It! panel, the children are encouraged to pray that the Holy Spirit fill them with power. This is a good time to lead spontaneous prayer asking for the Holy Spirit's power to help and guide them in a particular way.

## Written Prayer

Writing a response to God's Word can be especially effective for children who are more introverted and timid about speaking in front of others. Writing and drawing also give children a vehicle for processing their thoughts about what God is saying to them in Scripture. Children can pray through their writing and drawing in a variety of ways: They can write a letter to God, write their own prayer, write a poem, or draw a picture. (At the end of this chapter is the handout "A Letter to God" [Document #: TX003048] for children to use in writing letters to God. Using this page as a sample, you can make your own handout to work with any Featured Story in *The Catholic Children's Bible* or any Scripture passage you might choose.)

You may even encourage the children to put their creative writing and drawing into a prayer journal. A journal can be a child's collection of various expressions and communications with God. When you ask children to write a prayer or journal entry, it helps to be clear and direct about what they are to write. The Live It! panels of *The Catholic Children's Bible* Featured Story pages often offer specific suggestions for writing or drawing a response to a Scripture story.

For example, in the story of Samson (Featured Story "God Answers Samson's Prayer," in the Book of Judges), Samson asks God for strength. In the Live It! panel, the children respond to the story by writing their own prayer for strength. Similarly, in the story about Ruth and Naomi's friendship (Featured Story "Ruth Refuses to Leave Naomi," in the Book of Ruth), the children are asked to draw a picture of a friend and to ask God to bless this special friend. In some instances, the children are given the start to a prayer and asked to complete it.

## Meditation on Scripture

In meditation, children are invited to use their imagination to reflect on God's Word. This type of prayer is particularly effective with children at the fourth-grade level and older, as it often includes more abstract thinking. For example, many prayer leaders ask participants to relax the body, clear the mind, and breathe deeply before moving into meditation. Then, children might be guided into a meditation where they are asked to imagine Moses and the burning bush, Jesus' walking on water, or another of many stories that lend themselves to imaginative prayer. Through guided meditation, children have the opportunity not only to use their imaginations but also to be more attuned to God's message in stillness and quiet.

### *Lectio Divina*

*Lectio divina* is an ancient and very special type of scriptural prayer. Translated from Latin, it means "holy reading" or "spiritual reading." Here is a simplified version of the four steps of *lectio divina* that you can do with children.

1. *Lectio* (**Reading**) Proclaim the Scripture reading to the children. Read a portion of the reading, or a particular phrase, a second time and maybe even a third time.

   *Example:* Read John 10:11–15 (Featured Story "Jesus Is the Good Shepherd") in *The Catholic Children's Bible*. Then, slowly repeat the phrase "I am the Good Shepherd" two more times.

2. *Meditatio* (**Meditation**) Give the children a particular word or phrase to think about. Also, give a brief word of explanation as to why the chosen word or phrase is so important.

   *Example:* Explain what a shepherd is and show a picture of a shepherd. Then, ask the children to close their eyes and imagine Jesus as a good shepherd. Ask the children to silently reflect on the following question: How is Jesus like a shepherd in your life?

3. *Oratio* (**Prayer**) Ask the children to silently talk to God about the Word that they have heard.

   *Example:* "In the quiet of your heart, thank Jesus for being your Good Shepherd and talk to him about your family or your friends."

4. *Contemplatio* (**Contemplation**) Invite the children to be silent and rest in God's love.

*Example:* "Be still for one more minute and rest in the love and protection of the Good Shepherd."

## Silence and Scriptural Prayer

Children of any age are capable of silence and can greatly benefit from it. Of course, the amount of silent time must be in proportion to their age (about 1 minute for a second grader). Allowing time for silence, even at a young age, helps children to develop the habit of listening to God. It gives space and time for God's Word to take root and grow. Even though nothing "special" or out of the ordinary happens when children are silent, they do learn that silence is part of prayer. Thus, even the proclamation of the Word followed by one minute of silence can be a prayer.

All in all, scriptural prayer happens anytime we respond to God's Word. Having these various responses in your repertoire of prayer with Scripture can help you to introduce God's Word into the lives of the children you touch and will no doubt enrich your own experience of Scripture as well!

# A Letter to God

One way we can talk to God is by writing a letter. Read the story "A Lamb Saves God's People" (Exodus 12:21–23). Moses helped to keep the Israelites safe. Read the Live It! panel and then use this page to thank God for the people who keep you safe.

Dear God,

Love,

_____

(write your name here)

# Chapter 9

## Breaking Open the Word

## Understanding and Teaching Readings from Scripture

Helping children to understand God's Word is a vital part of the teacher's and catechist's role. This chapter provides you with a simple, surefire, time-tested method for helping children, and adults for that matter, to understand the Word of God.

We call this method breaking open Scripture or breaking open the Word. The "breaking open" means that we delve into, reflect on, and unpack the meaning of Scripture. Then we apply that meaning to our lives and respond in faith.

This method for breaking open Scripture is most often used with the Sunday Scripture readings. But this method can also be used with the weekday readings, the Featured Stories in *The Catholic Children's Bible*, or in any situation where we hear and reflect on the Word of God. As you lead the children in the methods outlined here, you will also find breaking open Scripture helpful to you personally. As you prepare to help children better understand Scripture, you will no doubt experience a deepening of your own understanding of God's Word.

We begin this section by clarifying a few of the terms that we will be using in this discussion.

## The Bible, Scripture, the Word of God, and the *Lectionary*

Without going into the nuances of the various terms, for our purposes, we must state that all three—the Bible, Scripture, and the Word of God—refer to God's inspired Word as recorded in the Bible. A term that is slightly less familiar is the *Lectionary*.

### The Lectionary

The *Lectionary* is the Church's liturgical book of Scripture readings. It contains the readings from the Bible that we hear at Mass on Sunday, on weekdays, on holy days, and at other liturgies. The lector and the presider use this book when proclaiming the readings at Mass. The Scripture readings are arranged in a very precise and particular order. The Church has chosen certain readings for the assembly to hear at certain times of the year, so we hear specific readings during Advent, Christmas, Lent, Easter, and

Ordinary Time. We hear the same readings every three years, because they are arranged in a three-year cycle: Year A, Year B, and Year C.

When we talk about breaking open Scripture, we are often referring to the breaking open of the Sunday Scripture readings, because the readings we hear on Sunday have a definite prominence in the Church's life. That's why they were chosen to be heard on Sunday by the whole assembly.

Furthermore, because the Sunday Scripture readings are especially significant and formative for our lives of faith, it is particularly important that we understand these holy texts, and that we help children to understand them. Thus, breaking open Sunday Scripture frequently occurs after Mass in a religious education setting. Or, for catechumens (the unbaptized who are preparing for the Sacraments) the breaking open of the Word occurs after they are dismissed from the Liturgy of the Word.

## The Proclamation

An important aspect to breaking open Scripture is the proclamation of the Word. There is something sacred about the actual proclamation of God's Word. Hearing God's Word proclaimed in the midst of the community of the faithful has a formative element not found when we read the Bible by ourselves. And we have the added benefit of the homily to help us understand the proclamation. Indeed, the homily is part of the Liturgy of the Word, and thereby part of the breaking open process. In addition to discussing the readings themselves, there may be discussion of, or questions about, the homily. The purpose of the homily is also to illuminate Scripture, albeit in a way that is different from breaking open the Word.

## Context and Time

There are several different contexts or settings in which to break open Sunday Scripture.

### On Sunday

Religious educators and liturgists alike tell us that reflecting on and discussing the Scripture we hear proclaimed at Mass is a faith-enriching process. A religious education class might meet right after Mass on a Sunday, in which case some of the children may have the reading fresh in their minds. Indeed, some children may have heard the Word proclaimed in a children's Liturgy of the Word, in which case they may have already begun to think about the meaning of God's Word. Usually, however, not all the children have been to Mass and thus another proclamation of the Word is needed.

## On a Weekday

Instead of meeting on Sunday, your children may meet for religious education on a weekday. Or, you may be a Catholic school teacher who also meets with her or his students during the week rather than on Sunday. In these cases, you will also need to proclaim the Sunday reading before you begin to break open Scripture.

## Dismissal with Catechumens

Another context for breaking open Sunday Scripture is during the dismissal catechesis for catechumens who are preparing for Baptism according to the *Rite of Christian Initiation of Adults*. In many parishes, children who participate in the RCIA are kindly dismissed after the homily to break open Scripture with a catechist.

## Other Occasions

There may be occasions when you simply gather your children and break open the Scripture readings you heard on Sunday. Or, you may want to "break open" a Scripture reading that was not part of Sunday liturgy. Maybe you just want to read a Bible story and talk about it in your Catholic school classroom, in your religious education setting, in your home, or anywhere else. You can use the process we provide here for that purpose too! In other words, breaking open Scripture does not have to be part of a larger religious education setting. It can stand alone.

## The Amount of Time It Takes

The amount of time you spend breaking open Scripture depends on the setting. If you are breaking open Sunday Scripture as part of a religious education class or a Catholic School religion class, you may spend only 10 to 15 minutes breaking open the Word before you move on to other topics. If, however, you are breaking open Sunday Scripture with young catechumens, you would spend 30 minutes or more. If you are doing this at home or in another setting, you could spend 10 to 30 minutes breaking open the readings.

The amount of time you have also affects how many of the readings you can break open. If you have 10 or 15 minutes, you will want to concentrate solely on the Gospel. We talk about the preeminence of the Gospel later. If you have more time, you may want to bring in the other readings as well as the homily.

Now that we have discussed the general notion of breaking open Sunday Scripture, we will move to the specific steps in the process.

# Breaking Open Sunday Scripture

Take a look at the following list of steps for breaking open Sunday Scripture, and get a feel for the flow. Then read the specific directions for each step. This process, in a formal setting, is called the Liturgy of the Word. However, this does not mean that it takes place in church. The Liturgy of the Word can be celebrated wherever we gather in the name of Jesus, because he is present with us in his Word.

## *The Liturgy of the Word*

**Opening comments**

**Proclamation of the Word**

**Silence**

**Initial question**

**Initial response from children**

**Brief exegesis (interpretation of Scripture as in the Understand It! panels of the Featured Stories in** *The Catholic Children's Bible***)**

**Deeper question**

**Second response from children**

**Pointing outward / Live It! (as in Featured Stories in** *The Catholic Children's Bible***)**

**Closing prayer**

The list of steps of the Liturgy of the Word provides you with an easy reference point, or template, to use anytime you break open Scripture. At the end of this section, you will find a reproducible template to use as you prepare to introduce a Scripture passage to the children (see the handout "Breaking Open the Word" [Document #: TX003049]).

Now, we will explain how to do each step and give you some examples.

**Liturgy of the Word**  The proclamation of the Word is the all-important first step. God is present in the Word and in the midst of the faithfully listening assembly. Sometimes the children may hear the Word proclaimed in the children's Liturgy of the Word. If you are breaking open a Scripture reading that was not part of the Sunday liturgy, begin with the next step.

**Opening comments**  As you begin the session, whether it's right after Mass or at another time, help the children to focus on the Word. Some initial remarks help the children to "tune in" to breaking open the Word. Depending on the setting, you may want to include an opening prayer or a gathering ritual.

For instance, let's say you are breaking open Sunday Scripture at the beginning of a religious education class that happens right after Mass on Sunday morning. Many, but not all, of the children heard the Gospel for the 31st Sunday in Ordinary Time, Year C, Luke 19:1–10, the story of Zacchaeus. You might begin your session with opening remarks like the following: "The reading for Mass today is the story of a short, little man named Zacchaeus. He was a rich, important man and also a tax collector. Tax collectors were not very popular and were sometimes even hated, because they collected people's money for the government. Notice what Zacchaeus does in the story."

**Proclamation of the Word**  Proclaim the reading from the Featured Story of *The Catholic Children's Bible* (or from the *Lectionary*). You may invite the children to read along with you in their Bibles. *The Catholic Children's Bible* provides extra helps to understanding, which will prove useful during the session. Allow for an extended period of silence (about 1 minute).

**Initial question**  The first question prompts children to share their initial response to the reading. The question connects with your opening remarks but is open-ended enough for various responses. Here are some examples:

- What did you notice about Zacchaeus in this story?
- What happened between Zacchaeus and Jesus?
- What was going on in this story?

**Initial response from children**  Give the children an opportunity to talk about what they found interesting in the story.

**Brief exegesis (interpretation of Scripture)**  Give the children some age-appropriate background information on Scripture to help them understand the reading. By doing this, you are teaching children scriptural interpretation from the Catholic perspective. The Understand It! panels of the Featured Stories in *The Catholic Children's Bible* provide age-appropriate interpretations of the reading. For further information and personal growth, you may want to look deeper into the readings by consulting any number of popular Scripture commentaries. Ask a parish staff person what is available at your parish.

Here is an example of how you might use the Understand It! panel of this story to offer an age-appropriate exegesis to the children: "In Jesus' day, much like today, it is an honor to have an important visitor in your home. So, the people in the story were probably shocked when a good person like Jesus said he would go to Zacchaeus's home.

People probably wondered why Jesus would go to this sinner's house. Jesus was trying to make a point by going to Zacchaeus's home."

**Deeper question** After you have guided the children to a better understanding of what is happening in the reading, ask them to think about the reading in light of this new information. You might ask some questions like these:

- Why do *you* think Jesus went to Zacchaeus's house?
- What message was Jesus giving Zacchaeus by going to his house? What message is Jesus giving us?

**Second response from children** Encourage the children to share their responses.

**Pointing outward / Live It!** Wrap up the children's responses and then direct them to look beyond themselves to how Jesus is calling us to live differently. Use the Live It! panel of the Featured Story to assist you with this step.

**Closing prayer** If the breaking open of Sunday Scripture is part of a larger session, you may want to save the closing prayer for the end of the session. If your session is concluding, repeat words and images from the Scripture reading for your closing prayer. You might say something like this: "Lord, Jesus, you called Zacchaeus to come down from the tree, and you call each of us too. Help us to answer your call and to follow you every day of our lives. We ask this in your name, for you live and reign forever and ever."

## How to Prepare for Breaking Open Sunday Scripture

Now that you have an idea of how to break open the Word with children, let's back up a step and discuss how you, the leader, prepare for this catechetical experience.

### Understanding the Liturgical Context

First, we must recognize that although breaking open Sunday Scripture may be a catechetical exercise, it is intimately connected to the Sunday liturgy, more specifically, to the Sunday Liturgy of the Word. Thus, as you begin to prepare, it is important to establish from the outset where we are in the liturgical year and how the readings fit within the Church's liturgical cycle.

For instance, John 21:1–14 is marvelous story about Jesus' helping the disciples catch a boatload of fish. When unpacking the meaning of this story, it is imperative to present it in the context of the Easter season and the Church's mission. That's part of the beauty and power of breaking open Sunday Scripture: The whole process begins with the Word as it is proclaimed in the Church's liturgy.

The Church's liturgy is the source and summit of our Catholic Christian life. Thus, when we break open Sunday Scripture, we are helping children to better understand the Word of God, the liturgy, and the life of the Church.

In order for you to help children better understand the Word as proclaimed in the liturgy, you must adequately prepare yourself with a prayerful heart and the right resources. We will give you the preparation steps and will name some of those helpful resources in the following section.

## Preparation Steps for the Leader

**Identify the Sunday readings.** You can find the Scripture readings for a particular Sunday in a number of places. Many parish bulletins list the Scripture readings for Sunday and for the weekdays. You can also find a listing of *Lectionary* readings for every day of the year at the USCCB Web site. A parish staff member could also help you to locate a paperback copy of the *Lectionary,* or even better, a resource that contains the *Lectionary* readings plus a reputable commentary on those readings, such as *At Home with the Word* (Liturgy Training Publications, 2010).

**Pray.** When you sit down to prepare for breaking open Sunday Scripture with children, begin with prayer. Ask the Holy Spirit to guide you as you reflect on the Word of God. Pray for the children with whom you will break open God's Word. Pray for openness to the Spirit and for wisdom in your preparations.

**Read the three *Lectionary* readings and the psalm.** Slowly and deliberately read each of the readings.

**Be silent.** Sit silently and let the Word resonate in your heart.

**Read the readings a second time.** As you read the second time, jot down the images, phrases, or words that stand out for you. Note what most strikes you in these readings.

**Name the insights.** Name any insights, messages, or questions that emerge for you.

**Read a commentary on the passage.** Broaden your personal interpretation of the passage by reading what Scripture scholars have to say. Better understanding the historical cultural context of the reading will give you a good foundation from which to discuss the passage with the children. Growing in knowledge of God's Word benefits not only the children's faith life but also your own. Then, once again, see what is available at your parish or use a source like *At Home with the Word*.

**Combine insights.** Meld your own insights with what the Scripture experts say about the reading. Does a theme, notion, or question emerge? Are you drawn to a particular image? What stands out now about the reading?

**Summarize.** Conclude the process by naming what God is saying to you and to the community. What is God's message? Being clear on God's message for you will help you as you now turn your attention to the children.

## Preparing for the Children

**Review the readings with children in mind.** Now that you have spent time with the readings, put on a new lens and then read the passages with an eye and ear for the children you teach. Imagine what characters, words, images, or phrases would stand out for a child. Determine what questions a child might have about a particular reading. What might be curious or difficult for an elementary school child?

For example, the Beatitudes (see Matthew 5:1–12) that we hear on the 4th Sunday in Ordinary Time, Year A, can be difficult for a child to understand. An elementary-age child may be unfamiliar with words and phrases like poor in spirit, meek, mourn, merciful, and righteousness. Keep this in mind, or write yourself a note as a reminder to review the terms with the children. Then move to the next step.

**Read the story from *The Catholic Children's Bible*.** Most of the Gospel stories and many of the readings from the Old and New Testaments can be found in the Featured Stories of *The Catholic Children's Bible*. Read not only the Scripture passage itself but also the Understand It! and Live It! panels that follow. This will help you to view the readings from the child's perspective.

Returning to the example of the Beatitudes, *The Catholic Children's Bible*, with the Good News Translation, puts the Beatitudes into simpler language for children. In addition, the Featured Story "Jesus Teaches Us How to Be Happy" highlights a manageable number of verses. Four Beatitudes (see Matthew 5:6–9) are emphasized, but, for further reading or discussion, the original nine are also referenced ("For the full story, read Matthew 5:3–12"). Thus *The Catholic Children's Bible* makes it easier to break open Sunday Scripture.

**Focus on the Gospel.** The Gospel is the preeminent reading among the three. Thus, when breaking open the Scripture readings, you usually focus first on the Gospel and then bring in the other readings as time allows. However, you may certainly find exceptions, and there may be times you choose to discuss the first or second reading also.

**Decide what to discuss with the children.** You have studied the readings and the commentaries. By now images and themes have emerged for you. Decide where the Spirit is leading you and what you will discuss with the children.

Returning to our example of the Beatitudes on 4th Sunday in Ordinary Time, Year A, you probably noticed that God's love for the poor and the lowly is a main theme throughout all the readings, including the psalm. Thus, God's love for the poor will likely be a theme you explore with the children when you break open the Scripture for this particular Sunday.

As you determine how you want to lead the children, you may find it helpful to use the handout "Breaking Open the Word" (Document #: TX003049), at the end of this chapter to put in writing the questions you will ask.

**Close with prayer.** Close your preparations with a prayer for the continued guidance of the Holy Spirit. Also think of the images and words you could use in a closing prayer with children. The following is an example of a prayer to end the breaking open of Sunday Scripture:

Let us pray. (Pause)

Lord Jesus,

You teach us the ways to happiness.

Help us to remember your Beatitudes

And to live them every day.

We ask this in your name, for you live and reign forever and ever.

Amen.

## Summary

Again, you may wish to refer to the handout "Breaking Open the Word" (Document #: TX003049), at the end of this chapter, for an outline of the "breaking open the Word" method. You may use this resource over and over as you prepare various Scripture passages for the children to read and understand.

In the next section, we offer some other activities that will help the children to engage with Scripture in both prayer and action.

# Breaking Open the Word

*Note to the teacher:* This resource is for your own use in preparing for breaking open the Word with children.

## The Liturgy of the Word

Opening comments

Proclamation of the Word (Featured Story)

Silence

Initial question

Initial response from children

Brief exegesis (Understand It! panel in Featured Story)

Deeper question

Second response from children

Pointing outward (Live It! panel in Featured Story)

Closing Prayer

Document #: TX003049

# Scripture Prayer and Activities Based on the Featured Stories

This is a hands-on section of handouts that can be used for specific Featured Stories in *The Catholic Children's Bible*. However, these handouts can also be used as templates for other Featured Stories or passages from Scripture. The following chart identifies each Scripture handout and the Featured Story or Stories each is based on, and offers a brief description of the activity or method of "breaking open the Word" used on the handout.

| Scripture Handout Title | Featured Story or Stories | Activity |
| --- | --- | --- |
| Handout "Great King David" (Document #: TX003051) | God Helps David to Defeat Goliath<br>David Brings the Ark of the Lord to Jerusalem | Filling in a chart on ways God helped David and helps me |
| Handout "The Story of Jeremiah" (Document #: TX003052) | God Chooses Jeremiah to Speak for Him | Outline of "breaking open the Word" for this story |
| Handout "A Kingdom Search" (Document #: TX003053) | None given for this handout | Children look up verses relating to the Kingdom of God |
| Handout "Jesus and Me" (Document #: TX003054) | Jesus Obeys His Parents | A Venn diagram |
| Handout "On the Road with Jesus" (Document #: TX003055) | Two Disciples Meet the Risen Jesus | A guided meditation |
| Handout "God's Armor" (Document #: TX003056) | Put On the Armor of God! | Filling in pieces of armor: How is God with me? |

# Great King David

There are many stories about King David in the Bible. God helped him to do many great things for the Kingdom of Israel. Read two of these stories, and start a list of the great things that King David did. Make a list of the great things God helps you do too!

Read the Featured Stories "God Helps David to Defeat Goliath" (1 Samuel 17:1–54) and "David Brings the Ark of the Lord to Jerusalem" (2 Samuel 6:12–19) in *The Catholic Children's Bible*. Then complete the chart.

| *God Helped David to . . .* | *God Helps Me to . . .* |
|---|---|
| ☐ *have courage* | ☐ *be strong when I'm afraid* |
| ☐ | ☐ |
| ☐ | ☐ |
| ☐ | ☐ |
| ☐ | ☐ |
| ☐ | ☐ |

**BONUS:** Read these other Featured Stories about David:
"Samuel Anoints David as the Future King" (1 Samuel 16:1–13)
"Jonathan Is a Good Friend to David" (1 Samuel 20:17–42)

Document #: TX003051

# The Story of Jeremiah

Prophets are people who speak for God. They give God's message. Read the story of the prophet Jeremiah in the Featured Story "God Chooses Jeremiah to Speak for Him" (Jeremiah 1:4–10) in *The Catholic Children's Bible.* Let's "break open" this Bible reading by thinking about it more deeply. Follow these steps:

**1.**
Read the passage again: Jeremiah 1:4–10.

**2.**
Be silent.

**3.**
What excuses did Jeremiah give to God?

_____

_____

_____

**4.**
Read the Understand It! panel in *The Catholic Children's Bible.*

**5.**
What did God promise Jeremiah?

_____

_____

What did God promise you?

_____

_____

_____

**6.**
How will you be a "prophet" this week in school? At home?

_____

_____

_____

Document #: TX003052

# A Kingdom Search

Go on a Bible search in *The Catholic Children's Bible* and find out what the Kingdom of God is like. You can find clues in both the Old Testament and the New Testament. Read these passages:

- Isaiah 11:6–9
  *Hint:* Find the "Prophets" color band (orange) at the bottom of the page and then look for the purple color tab to find the Book of Isaiah.

- Matthew 13:44–46
  *Hint:* Find the "Gospels" color band (blue) at the bottom of the page and then look for the aqua color tab to find Matthew.

- Matthew 19:13–15
  *Hint:* Find the color band of the "Gospels" and the color tab for the Gospel of Matthew as you did above.

Now, in the space below, write phrases or words, or draw pictures, that describe the Kingdom of God. This has been started for you.

**The Kingdom of God is like . . .**

No fighting

Document #: TX003053

# Jesus and Me

Jesus was once a child just like you. Read the Featured Story "Jesus Obeys His Parents" (Luke 2:41–52) in *The Catholic Children's Bible*, about Jesus when he was a boy. Then read more about the story in the Understand It! panel. Think about ways that you and Jesus are alike and different, and fill out the Venn diagram below. In the center section, write things about you and Jesus that are the same. Then fill in the spaces for "Jesus as a child" and "Me as a child." Some examples have been started for you.

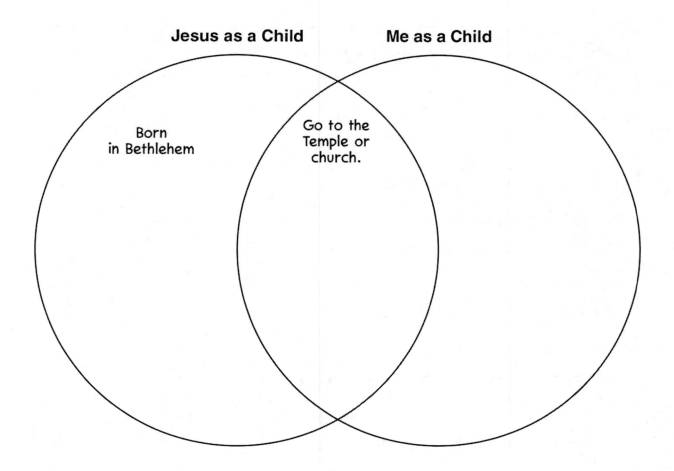

**Jesus as a Child**            **Me as a Child**

Born
in Bethlehem

Go to the
Temple or
church.

# On the Road with Jesus

Try this meditation on the Gospel. Your teacher or parent can lead you through it, or you may do it by yourself. The first thing to do is read the Featured Story "Two Disciples Meet the Risen Jesus" (Luke 24:13–35) in *The Catholic Children's Bible*. Then think over the story again, and imagine yourself with Jesus and the two disciples. Read each line, and close your eyes for a moment to imagine what it says. Then read the next line. If you like, write down your thoughts or draw what you imagine.

Picture the path that you and a friend are walking along as you talk. . . .

_____

Imagine that someone joins you and walks along with you. . . .

_____

Imagine that it's getting dark outside. . . .

_____

So, the three of you go to a house. Picture the house. . . .

_____

Picture the three of you sitting down together. . . .

_____

The "stranger" takes some bread and breaks it. . . .

_____

Aha! You recognize that this person is Jesus! He disappears.

_____

Imagine what you say to your friend about Jesus. . . .

_____

Now, in your heart, what would you like to tell Jesus yourself?

_____

# God's Armor

In the Letter to the Ephesians, Saint Paul tells us to put on God's armor to protect ourselves from evil. Read Saint Paul's letter in the Featured Story "Put On the Armor of God!" (Ephesians 6:10–18) in *The Catholic Children's Bible.* Next, read the Understand It! panel and fill in each piece of armor by giving an example from your life. To help you get started, we have given you two examples.

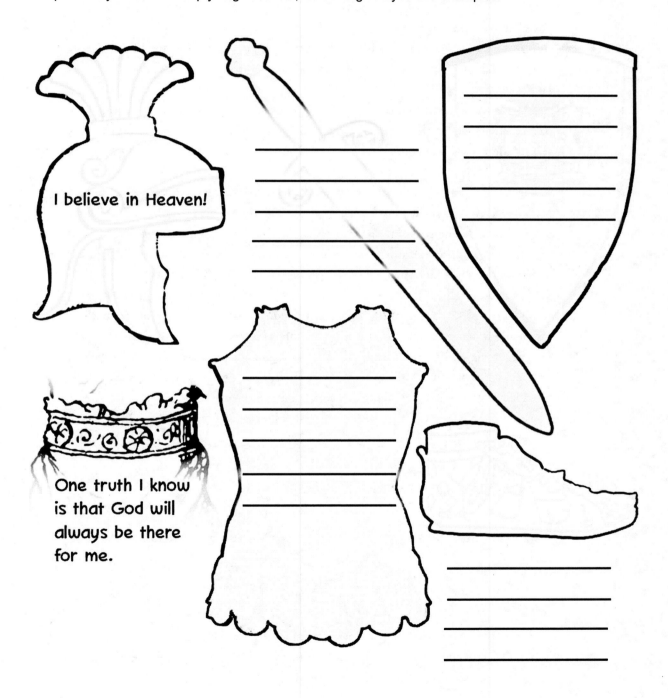

I believe in Heaven!

One truth I know is that God will always be there for me.

Document #: TX003056

# Chapter 10

## Scripture through the Year, in Prayer and Activities

For Catholics, the year revolves around the feasts and seasons of the liturgical year. From Advent to Easter, we journey with the liturgy through the events of the life of Christ, and, through our participation in Word and Sacrament, we unite with him in the here-and-now.

In the liturgy, both the past and the future are present, because in the liturgy we participate in the timelessness and eternity of God. The Scripture readings for each season and each feast help us to understand the particular grace that this season or this day brings to us.

In this chapter, the Scripture readings for some of the most important seasons and feasts are presented in two ways. First, the readings are presented in the context of an opening and closing prayer for a celebratory classroom session for a particular season or feast. The Scripture readings are, in most cases, based on the actual readings found in the *Lectionary*, with the comparable Featured Story from *The Catholic Children's Bible* noted as well. This opening and closing prayer is offered in a handout format to facilitate the participation of the children. In addition, a Ritual Guide on the back of the handout can guide you in preparing for these prayers and in leading the children through them. Second, following each handout, a hands-on activity based on the season or feast is also presented. Taken together, these two resources (prayer and activity) provide ample material for a religious education session.

Prayers and activities are provided for the following seasons and feasts:

- All Saints' Day (November 1)
- Advent
- Our Lady of Guadalupe (December 12)
- Christmas
- Epiphany
- The Baptism of Jesus
- Ordinary Time
- Lent
- The Annunciation of Mary (March 25)
- Palm Sunday
- The Easter Triduum
- The Easter Season
- Pentecost

Look through these scriptural prayer sessions and activities as you plan your year. You may find something that will help you to communicate and celebrate the meaning of a particular season or feast with your children.

# Prayers for All Saints' Day

**Scripture Focus:** Matthew 5:8–9 (Featured Story "Jesus Teaches Us How to Be Happy")

## Opening Prayer

**Leader:** Let us begin our prayer with the Sign of the Cross.
**All:** In the name of the Father . . .
**Leader:** In this Gospel passage, God tells us that we will see him if we turn our hearts toward him, and that we are his children when we work for peace.
**Reader:** A reading from the holy Gospel according to Matthew.
*Reader then reads the Scripture passage above from* The Catholic Children's Bible.
**Leader:** As we pray, let us respond by saying together, "Amen!"
**All:** Amen!
**Leader:** Turn our hearts to you, O God, and help us to follow you.
**All:** Amen!
**Leader:** Give us peace in our hearts, O God.
**All:** Amen!
**Leader:** Help us to share your peace with everyone we meet.
**All:** Amen! Amen! Amen!

## Closing Prayer

**Leader:** Today we learned to follow in the footsteps of Jesus, just like the saints. When we pray, we pray with all the saints in Heaven! Let us pray a prayer of praise with all the saints by repeating after me:
**Leader:** Holy, holy, holy!
**All:** Holy, holy, holy!
**Leader:** Jesus, you are the Holy One.
**All:** Jesus, you are the Holy One.
**Leader:** Help us to follow you.
**All:** Help us to follow you.
**Leader:** We ask in your name. Amen!
**All:** We ask in your name. Amen!

Document #: TX003057

# Ritual Guide

## Opening Prayer

### Preparation

Choose a reader to read the passage from the Gospel of Matthew.

*Optional:* You may want to choose an appropriate song to begin or end the prayer.

### Gather

Gather the children in the Bible corner. Distribute the prayer handouts. Briefly rehearse the prayer response, noting that the group will say "Amen" once for the first two petitions and three times for the last petition. Remind the children that *Amen* means "So be it" or "I agree."

### Pray

Begin with the Sign of the Cross as indicated. Introduce the reading with the words given for the Leader, or in your own words. After the prayer, collect the prayer handouts. They will not be needed for the closing prayer.

(An activity for All Saints' Day can be found on page 63 of *The Catholic Children's Bible Leader Guide*.)

## Closing Prayer

### Preparation

This prayer is based on the activity offered for All Saints' Day. However, if you did not offer this activity, you can adapt the introduction to summarize the main point of the day's lesson.

### Gather

Gather the children in the Bible corner. Explain that the closing prayer is a prayer asking Jesus to help us follow him. (Because this is a repetitive prayer, the children will not need their handouts.)

Tell the children that you will be the leader and that they should repeat each line after you.

### Pray

Lead the children in prayer.

*Optional:* You may want to end with the song you chose for the opening prayer.

Document #: TX003057

# Activity for All Saints' Day

## Stepping Along Happiness Lane

**Scripture Focus:** Matthew 5:8–9 (Featured Story "Jesus Teaches Us How to Be Happy"). The children learn that we are saints in the making in God's family and, like the saints, we can work for peace.

**Gather the following items:** two or three templates of a footprint; construction paper, scissors, and crayons or markers, one of each for each student
*Optional:* 12-inch sticks or rulers (one for each child), tape

**Let's Look It Up!** Have the children open *The Catholic Children's Bible* to the Gospel of Matthew in the New Testament. Direct them to find chapter 5, verses 8–9. Explain that this is part of a Gospel story that we hear at Mass. In this passage, Jesus teaches us about happiness. (*Note:* Consider making the Featured Story "Jesus Teaches Us How to Be Happy" the basis for your lesson.)

## Activity

1. Give each child a sheet of construction paper, a crayon or marker, and a pair of scissors. Direct the children to share the footprint templates and to each trace it on their paper and carefully cut it out. Assign each child one word (or more, depending upon group size) from Matthew 5:8–9 to write on his or her footprint. Cut out an extra footprint, and on it write out the following Scripture verse and citation: "Happy are the pure in heart; they will see God! Happy are those who work for peace; God will call them his children!" (Matthew 5:8–9). As a class, have the children arrange their footprints on the floor, perhaps around the classroom, in the correct word order according to the Scripture passage.

   To add a pennant to this activity, continue with step 2. If you will not be having the children make the pennant, close the activity here by asking the children to step along (not on!) their "Happiness Lane" as they read the Beatitudes together. (*Optional:* You may want to play a recording of instrumental music as the children continue stepping around the room.)

2. To make the pennant, distribute to each child a new sheet of construction paper and a 12-inch stick or ruler. Instruct the children to cut out a large triangle or pennant shape. They should label the top "Saint in the Making" and then draw a self-portrait underneath it. On the back of the pennant, direct them to write their first name and their birth date. Then ask them to write and complete this sentence:

"I can be a peacemaker by . . ." Provide tape to attach pennant to the stick or ruler. (Remind the children to handle the sticks or rulers carefully and to keep them away from their own and others' faces!)

3. Call on the children to share their peacemaking ideas and their self-portrait pennants. Invite them to process along "Happiness Lane" with their pennants. You might want to have the children sing a song as they process ("When the Saints Go Marching In" works well). Display the pennants along "Happiness Lane" as a reminder that we all are members of God's family who, like the saints, can follow Jesus and be peacemakers.

# Prayers for Advent

**Scripture Focus:** Philippians 4:4–9 (Featured Story "Rejoice and Give Thanks")

## Opening Prayer

**Leader:** Let us begin our prayer with the Sign of the Cross.

**All:** In the name of the Father . . .

**Leader:** In this passage, Saint Paul tells us to be happy and rejoice, because Jesus is coming soon. We can welcome him with thankful hearts.

**Reader:** A reading from Saint Paul's Letter to the Philippians.

*Reader then reads the Scripture passage above from* The Catholic Children's Bible.

**Leader:** As we ask Jesus for what we need, let us pray together: "We rejoice and are glad."

**All:** We rejoice and are glad.

**Leader:** Lord Jesus, with thankful hearts we ask for your peace during this Advent season.

**All:** We rejoice and are glad.

**Leader:** Lord Jesus, we ask to have a gentle attitude toward everyone as we prepare for your coming at Christmas.

**All:** We rejoice and are glad.

**Leader:** Lord Jesus, we pray for our needs, and for the needs of those we know and love, especially for . . . [invite the children to name people or situations they wish to pray for].

**All:** We rejoice and are glad.

## Closing Prayer

**Leader:** Today we learned ways to help others during the season of Advent. Let us pray for the needs of all God's people, especially for those who feel lonely and forgotten. Let us pray together:

**All:** Lord Jesus,

As we prepare to celebrate your coming to the world at Christmas, we pray for the needs of all people.

Give peace to our world. Give food to the hungry. Give shelter to those who are homeless. Help mothers and fathers and newborn babies. Help all the children everywhere.

Help us find ways to help others in need.

We ask this in your name, Lord Jesus, who came to us as a little child.

Amen.

# Ritual Guide

## Opening Prayer

### Preparation

Choose a reader (or three readers, one for each verse) to read the passage from the Letter to the Philippians.
*Optional:* You may want to choose an appropriate Advent song to begin or end the prayer. (Suggestion: "O Come, O Come, Emmanuel.")

### Gather

Gather the children in the Bible corner. Distribute the prayer handouts. Briefly rehearse the prayer response, pointing out that we will hear a similar phrase in the Scripture reading.

### Pray

If you are using an Advent wreath, you may light the appropriate candle(s) on the wreath at this time. Begin with the Sign of the Cross as indicated. Introduce the reading with the words given, or in your own words. At the close of this prayer, collect the prayer handouts and set them aside, as they will be needed for the closing prayer.
(An activity for Advent can be found on page 67 of *The Catholic Children's Bible Leader Guide*.)

## Closing Prayer

### Preparation

This prayer is based on the activity offered for Advent. However, if you did not offer this activity, you can adapt the introduction to summarize the main point of the day's lesson.

### Gather

Gather the children in the Bible corner. Explain that in the closing prayer, we will follow Saint Paul's advice in today's reading and ask God for what we need. Explain that at "All," we will read the prayer together.

### Pray

Lead the children in prayer.
*Optional:* You may want to end with the song you chose for the opening prayer.

# Activity for Advent

## Linking to Others

**Scripture Focus:** Philippians 4:4–7 (Featured Story "Rejoice and Give Thanks"). The children will plan and prepare to celebrate the birth of Jesus. They will decide on ways to help others during the four weeks of Advent.

**Gather the following items: multicolored** construction paper, two sheets for each child; scissors, one for each child; a stapler, tape or glue, a ball of string, and a hole punch

**Let's Look It Up!** Have the children open *The Catholic Children's Bible* to Saint Paul's Letter to the Philippians in the New Testament. Direct them to find chapter 4, verses 4–7. Explain that this passage tells how prayer helps us and guides us on how to treat others. (*Note:* Consider making the Featured Story "Rejoice and Give Thanks" the basis for your lesson.)

## Activity

1. (This activity can be an individual activity—four links with four paper ornaments, or a class activity—twenty-four links with twenty-four paper ornaments.) Make a paper link chain. Distribute multicolored construction paper and scissors, and explain to the children that they will be making a paper chain. Direct the children to fold their papers vertically into four strips that are each two inches wide. Then instruct them to cut on the folds to make four equal strips.

   Show the children how to bend the strips to form a circle. Have them staple, tape, or glue the edges together. Demonstrate how to bend and feed the second strip through the first link and fasten the ends together to form the second link. Explain that the students will repeat this procedure to create four links. Before connecting the fourth link, invite the children to join their links together to make a class paper chain.

2. Distribute another sheet of construction paper to each child. Demonstrate how to fold the paper to make four equal boxes. Instruct the children to cut out four paper ornaments. Suggest that they cut out basic geometric shapes—circle, square, triangle, diamond—or they can draw a bell, star, or angel.

3. Gather the children together for a brainstorming session. Ask the class to think of ways they can prepare for Jesus' birth during the four weeks of Advent. Direct them

to focus on family or home, friend or neighbor, parish, and community. Ask: What can you do to help others during Advent? Write their ideas on a whiteboard. Then invite the children to choose what they will do each week (or each of the twenty-four days) and to write their choices on their ornaments.

4. Invite the children to bring their ornaments for the first week of Advent to add to the class chain. Using a hole punch and string, show the children how to attach their ornaments to one of the links on the chain. Display the Advent class chain in your prayer corner. Each week invite the children to add another ornament and share with the class what they did for others that week. Use the Advent class chain as garland on the class Christmas tree.

# Prayers for the Feast of Our Lady of Guadalupe

**Scripture Focus:** Luke 1:41–42

## Opening Prayer

**Leader:** Let us begin our prayer with the Sign of the Cross. In the name of the Father . . .

**Leader:** Today we honor Mary under her title Our Lady of Guadalupe. In this reading, God tells us that Mary is especially blessed because she brought Jesus into the world.

**Reader:** A reading from the holy Gospel according to Luke.

*Reader then reads the Scripture passage above from* The Catholic Children's Bible.

**Leader:** We ask Mary to pray for us because she is so close to Jesus. Let's honor Mary together! Let's tell her, over and over, "Blessed are you, Mary."

**All:** Blessed are you, Mary.

**Leader:** Mary, Our Lady of Guadalupe, you are the mother of Jesus.

**All:** Blessed are you, Mary.

**Leader:** Mary, Our Lady of Guadalupe, you are our mother too!

**All:** Blessed are you, Mary.

**Leader:** Mary, Our Lady of Guadalupe, you are the patroness of all the Americas: North America, Central America, and South America!

**All:** Blessed are you, Mary.

**Leader:** We love you and honor you as our mother always.

**All:** Blessed are you, Mary.

## Closing Prayer

**Leader:** Today we honored Mary under her title of Our Lady of Guadalupe. Let us thank her for all her love and care for us:

**All:** Thank you, Mary, for loving us as your children, the brothers and sisters of Jesus.

Thank you for the beautiful picture you left on the cloak of Juan Diego.

Thank you for the beautiful roses you left as a sign.

Pray for all of us, your children of the Americas.

Amen.

# Ritual Guide

## Opening Prayer

### Preparation

Find a picture, even a small holy card, of Our Lady of Guadalupe to place in the Bible corner. You may also want to have a map available to point out North America, Central America, and South America. Choose a reader to read the passage from the Gospel of Luke.
*Optional:* You may wish to choose an appropriate Marian hymn or song to begin or end the prayer.

### Gather

Gather the children in the Bible corner. Point out the picture of Our Lady of Guadalupe, and explain that we are honoring her especially today. Using the map, if possible, show the children North America, Central America, and South America. Ask if children have family members living in any of these countries. Distribute the prayer handouts. Briefly rehearse the prayer response, noting that it comes from the Gospel reading we will be hearing.

### Pray

Begin with the Sign of the Cross as indicated. Introduce the reading with the words given, or in your own words. Collect the prayer handouts and set them aside for the closing prayer.
(An activity for the Feast of Our Lady of Guadalupe can be found on page 71 of *The Catholic Children's Bible Leader Guide.*)

## Closing Prayer

### Preparation

This prayer is based on the story of the appearance of Our Lady of Guadalupe to Juan Diego.

### Gather

Gather the children in the Bible corner. Explain that in this prayer we are thanking Mary for her love and concern for the people of the Americas. Point out the picture of Our Lady of Guadalupe and, if possible, the Americas on the map.

### Pray

Lead the children in prayer.
*Optional:* You may want to end with the song you chose for the opening prayer.

# Activity for Our Lady of Guadalupe

## Honoring Mary with Roses

**Scripture Focus:** Luke 1:41–42. The children will deepen their knowledge and appreciation of ways to honor Mary as Our Lady of Guadalupe.

**Gather the following items:** a roll of brown craft paper or brown material to resemble a cloak (a sheet may be used); scissors; string or wool (optional); four large sheets of red tissue paper for each child; a stapler; green pipe cleaners, one for each child; a large illustration of Our Lady of Guadalupe; and large safety pins, one for each child

**Let's Look It Up!** Have the children open their Bibles to the Gospel of Luke in the New Testament. Direct them to find chapter 1, verses 41–42. Explain that this passage is part of a prayer that we pray to Mary to honor her.

## Activity

1. Together with the children, make a tilma by cutting a 40-inch length of brown paper and folding it in half lengthwise. Cut a 7-inch circle in the middle at the top. Fringe the bottom with scissors or punch holes and tie with colored string or wool. Glue the picture of Our Lady to the front of the tilma. Then attach safety pins around the entire image. Hang the tilma in the Bible corner.

2. Distribute four sheets of tissue paper to each child. You may use any color, although red is preferred. Have the children fold the sheets in half and cut to make eight sheets of 10-x-13-inch paper. (You may prepare by cutting the sheets prior to the distribution.) Explain that they are to stack all eight sheets of tissue paper in a neat pile.

3. Holding the stack with the shorter side at the top, demonstrate how to fold the tissue paper back and forth, forming a 1-inch accordion. When the sheets are folded, have the children trim the corners slightly to form a rounded shape.

4. Show the children how to pinch the accordion-folded paper in the middle and wrap the green pipe cleaner securely around the middle of the folded tissue paper. Bend the two ends together after attaching the pipe cleaner. You might want to use a staple to hold the folds of the two sides upright and together.

5. Explain to the children that now they are to carefully separate and fluff the tissue paper sheets, layer by layer. This will make a large, fluffy rose.

6. Gather the children for a procession to the Bible corner holding their roses. You may want to play a recording of a hymn to Mary.

7. As the children approach the Bible corner, invite each child to slip his or her rose through a safety pin that has been attached around Mary's image on the paper or material. When every rose is attached, together pray a Hail Mary.

# Prayers for Christmas

**Scripture Focus:** Luke 2:1–20 (Featured Story "Shepherds Announce the Good News of Jesus' Birth")

## Opening Prayer

**Leader:** Let us begin our prayer with the Sign of the Cross.
**All:** In the name of the Father . . .
**Leader:** In this Gospel, we learn that after Jesus was born, Mary placed him in a manger, because there was no room for them in the inn.
**Reader:** A reading from the holy Gospel according to Luke.
*Reader then reads the Scripture passage above from* The Catholic Children's Bible.
**Leader:** This Christmas, let us make room for Jesus in our hearts. Let us pray, "Come to our hearts, Lord Jesus."
**All:** Come to our hearts, Lord Jesus.
**Leader:** When we prepare for your coming by listening to our parents, guardians, and teachers,
**All:** Come to our hearts, Lord Jesus.
**Leader:** When we show kindness to others, especially to members of our own families,
**All:** Come to our hearts, Lord Jesus.
**Leader:** When we celebrate Christmas with our families and friends,
**All:** Come to our hearts, Lord Jesus.
**Leader:** When we participate in the Holy Mass on Christmas,
**All:** Come to our hearts, Lord Jesus.

## Closing Prayer

**Leader:** When we celebrate Christmas, we celebrate that Jesus came to us as a poor little baby. Help us to remember that, of all the gifts we receive at Christmas, Jesus is the best Gift of all.
**Leader:** Please repeat each line after me.

Poor little Jesus

Born in a stable

Help me to love you

Best as I am able.

Help me to serve you

In one another.

Help me to love *all*

As sisters and brothers.

Amen!

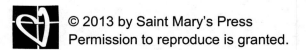

# Ritual Guide

## Opening Prayer

### Preparation

Choose a reader to read the passage from the Gospel of Luke.
*Optional:* You may want to choose an appropriate song to begin or end the prayer. (Suggestion: "Silent Night" or another Christmas carol.)

### Gather

Gather the children in the Bible corner. Distribute the prayer handouts. Briefly rehearse the prayer response.

### Pray

Begin with the Sign of the Cross as indicated. Introduce the reading with the words given for the leader, or in your own words. Collect the prayer handouts. As the closing prayer is a repetitive prayer, the children will not need them again.
(An activity for Christmas can be found on page 75 of *The Catholic Children's Bible Leader Guide*.)

## Closing Prayer

### Preparation

This prayer, while based on the activity offered for Christmas, is suitable for any activity or celebration of Christmas.

### Gather

Gather the children in the Bible corner. Explain that our closing prayer reminds us that Jesus wants us to love him, ourselves, and others. (Because this is a repetitive prayer, the children will not need their handout sheets.) Tell the children that you will be the leader and that they should repeat each line after you.

### Pray

Lead the children in prayer.
*Optional:* You may want to end with the Christmas carol you chose for the opening prayer, or a different one.

Document #: TX003060

# Activity for Christmas

## Come, Lord Jesus!

**Scripture Focus:** Luke 2:6–7 (Featured Story "Shepherds Announce the Good News of Jesus' Birth"). The children will come to appreciate the Christmas story by making a replica of the Christmas crib to take home with them.

**Gather the following items:** a manger scene set up in the classroom; shoeboxes*, one for each child; a handful of straw for each child; balls of plastic clay that can be colored with markers, one or more for each child; and markers, several for each child

**Let's Look It Up!** Have the children open *The Catholic Children's Bible* to the Gospel of Luke in the New Testament. Direct them to find chapter 2, verses 6–7. Explain that in this passage we learn that Jesus was born in a manger—a large wooden box that holds food for animals. (*Note:* Consider making the Featured Story "Shepherds Announce the Good News of Jesus' Birth" the basis for your lesson.)

## Activity

1. Gather the children in front of the manger scene, and ask them to look at it carefully. Ask the children to tell what they know about the figures in the scene.

2. Explain that the children will be making manger scenes to take home. Give each child a shoebox for the stable, some straw for the manger and the floor, some plastic clay, and some markers. (The amount of clay will depend on how many figures they will make. Jesus, the manger, Mary, and Joseph are essential. Shepherds, sheep, and angels can be added if there is enough clay.)

3. Discuss briefly who belongs in the scene. Direct the children to begin making their clay figures. When they are finished and the clay is dry, the children can color the figures with markers. Remind the children that they can draw windows (open to the stars) and doors on the interior of their stables. They might like to draw animals in the stalls as well.

4. When all have finished, have a "room tour" so that everyone can see and admire the manger scenes. Close the session by gathering the children in the Bible corner or before the manger scene and singing "Silent Night."

*If you are planning to do the activity for the Baptism of Jesus after Christmas, you may want to save the shoebox lids.

# Prayers for Epiphany

**Scripture Focus:** Matthew 2:9–11: (Featured Story: "Jesus Birth Was Special")

## Opening Prayer

**Leader:** Let us begin our prayer with the Sign of the Cross.
**All:** In the name of the Father . . .
**Leader:** In this Gospel, we hear about some people who saw a star that led them to a special child. Those people were the Three Kings, and the special child was Jesus.
**Reader:** A reading from the holy Gospel according to Matthew.
*Reader then reads the Scripture passage above from* The Catholic Children's Bible.
**Leader:** Today we celebrate the Feast of Epiphany, the Three Kings, who found Jesus and worshipped him. Let's do what they did right now. First, everyone please stand up and face the Christmas crib. After each prayer, say the response, "We kneel down and worship you." Then kneel on both knees for a minute until I begin the next prayer.
**Leader:** Lord Jesus, thank you for coming among us as God and man. Thank you for becoming a little child. Thank you for showing yourself to the Three Kings.
**All:** We kneel down and worship you.
*All kneel for a moment.*
**Leader:** Lord Jesus, thank you for choosing Mary and Joseph as your mother and foster father. They helped you to learn and to grow. Thank you for our parents, grandparents, and guardians, who help us to learn and to grow.
**All:** We kneel down and worship you.
*All kneel for a moment.*
**Leader:** Lord Jesus, thank you for sending the star to guide the Three Kings. Thank you for our Pope and bishops, our pastors, our deacons, and our teachers, and all who guide us to you.
**All:** We kneel down and worship you.
*All kneel for a moment.*

## Closing Prayer

**Leader:** Today we learned that the Three Kings found Jesus, and that Jesus came for everyone. Let's ask the Three Kings to lead us in prayer:
**King 1:** Jesus is our King. I brought him gold, my most precious possession.
**All:** Jesus, we give you our hearts.
**King 2:** Jesus is our God. I brought him incense, a sign of my heartfelt worship.
**All:** Jesus, we worship you.
**King 3:** Jesus died and is now risen. I brought him myrrh, to anoint his body. And now he lives forever!
**All:** Jesus, you died and rose for us. You are with us now. Alleluia!

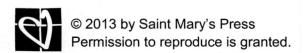 Document #: TX003061

# Ritual Guide

## Opening Prayer

### Preparation

Choose a reader to read the passage from the Gospel of Matthew.
*Optional:* You may want to choose an appropriate song to begin or end the prayer. (Suggestion: "We Three Kings")

### Gather

Gather the children before the Christmas crib. Distribute the prayer handouts. Briefly rehearse the prayer response and then practice kneeling and standing again quietly.

### Pray

Begin with the Sign of the Cross as indicated. Introduce the reading with the words given, or in your own words.
(An activity for Epiphany can be found on page 79 of *The Catholic Children's Bible Leader Guide.*)

## Closing Prayer

### Preparation

This prayer is based on the story of the Three Kings as told in the Gospel of Matthew. Choose three children to be the Three Kings. You may have paper crowns for them to wear, or large name tags labeled "King 1," "King 2," and "King 3" to identify them as kings. You may give them small boxes to carry as gifts, or ask them to pretend to carry a gift. Gather the kings, standing, in one spot and have each step forward separately to read his or her line. Remind them to lay their gifts (boxes or their "pretend gifts") at the feet of Jesus in the Christmas Nativity scene after they speak. They may then join the group.

### Gather

Gather the children at the Christmas crib and ask them to sit down. Distribute the prayer handouts. Explain that the Three Kings will lead us in our closing prayer today.

### Pray

Motion each king forward to speak his or her line.
*Optional:* You may want to end with the song you chose for the opening prayer.

# Activity for Epiphany

## Gift for a King from a King

**Scripture Focus:** Matthew 2:9–11 (Featured Story "Jesus' Birth Was Special"). The children will make a mural to illustrate the Epiphany story.

**Gather the following items:** four sheets of poster board, four sets of markers or crayons (*optional:* paints, paintbrushes), drawing paper, three camel templates and three king templates, three pairs of scissors, and three bottles of glue

**Let's Look It Up!** Have the children open *The Catholic Children's Bible* to the Gospel of Matthew in the New Testament. Direct them to find chapter 2, verses 9–11. Explain that this is part of the Gospel story about the three kings traveling with gifts for the Baby Jesus. (*Note:* Consider making the Featured Story "Jesus' Birth Was Special" the basis for your lesson.)

## Activity

1. You may wish to do this activity over two sessions. In the first session, the background scenes will be drawn and colored. In the second session, each of three groups will draw a king, a camel, and a gift. (If time permits, the entire mural can be drawn and painted in one session.)

2. In the first session, divide the class into three groups of four to eight children and distribute a sheet of poster board and markers or crayons to each group. Explain that each group will be drawing a panel of a mural based on the Epiphany story as follows, with color suggestions: (1) the desert (sand color), (2) hills in the background (purple), and (3) the final destination (brown stable with a yellow star over it). When the scene is completed, hang it in the prayer corner. (If you have a larger group, more desert scenes and hill scenes can be added to make a longer mural.)

3. In the second session, divide the class into three groups, and distribute drawing paper, a king and camel template, a scissors, and crayons or markers to each. Assign one group to be the "gold" group, one to be the "frankincense" group, and one to be the "myrrh" group. Brainstorm with each of these groups what they need to draw and which colors to use to complete the scene of the visit of the kings, including camels (brown), saddles and reins (red), and their individual gifts. Have the kings represent different ethnicities—white, black, and brown skin tones. Suggest that

each king be dressed in different royalty colors (such as purple, red, gold or yellow). Distribute the camel and king templates for the children to use to aid their drawing.

4. Distribute a pair of scissors and a bottle of glue to each group. Explain to the groups that after they have drawn and colored their part of the scene, they should carefully cut out the king, camel, and gift. When all have finished, direct each group to attach its king and camel to part of the three-panel scene.

5. When the three groups have attached their parts to the scene, ask a representative from each group to hold the drawn gift box. Gather the children together and ask them what *they* would like to bring to the Baby Jesus. On each of the gift boxes, have each child in each group write what gift he or she would give to Jesus.

6. Invite the "gold" group to process around the room to the stable. Then invite the representative to attach the gift at the stable. Continue in the same way for the "frankincense" and "myrrh" groups. As the children process, have them join in singing "We Three Kings." If the lyrics are available, have each group sing the appropriate verse for its specific gift.

# Prayers for the Baptism of Jesus

**Scripture Focus:** Matthew 3:13–17 (Featured Story "Jesus Obeys His Heavenly Father")

## Opening Prayer

**Leader:** Let us begin our prayer with the Sign of the Cross.

**All:** In the name of the Father . . .

**Leader:** When Jesus was baptized, something very special happened. The Holy Spirit came down upon Jesus, and God the Father said that he was very pleased with his Son, Jesus.

**Reader:** A reading from the holy Gospel according to Matthew.

*Reader then reads the Scripture passage above from* The Catholic Children's Bible.

**Leader:** When we were baptized, we became children of God and brothers and sisters of Jesus. The Holy Spirit came to live in us. Let us respond in prayer with thanks to God our Father, to Jesus our Lord and Brother, and to the Holy Spirit:

God our Father, thank you for making us your children in Baptism, and making us brothers and sisters of Jesus. Help us to please you in all that we do.

**All:** Thank you, God our Father.

**Leader:** Jesus our Lord and Brother, thank you for coming to live among us as God and man. Help us to love one another as you have commanded.

**All:** Thank you, Jesus, our Lord and Brother.

**Leader:** Holy Spirit of God, thank you for coming to live in us through Baptism and again, in a stronger way, in Confirmation. Be with us to lead us and guide us in right paths.

**All:** Thank you, Holy Spirit.

## Closing Prayer

**Leader:** Let's sit down and fold our hands in our laps. Today we learned to pray with Jesus in the desert. Sometimes we can pray better when all is quiet and still. Let us be quiet and still for a moment, and pray to Jesus in our hearts. *[Allow a few moments for the children to sit in stillness.]*

**Leader:** When Jesus was baptized, God our Father said that he was pleased. When God sees that we try to be good and to care for others, he is pleased with us too. Let us stay quiet and listen as I go to each of you. Everyone should say "Amen" after I say the prayer each time. *[Go to each child, put one hand on the child's head, and say, "This is (name), with whom God our Father is pleased." **All** respond each time: "Amen."]*

# Ritual Guide

## Opening Prayer

Choose a reader to read the passage from the Gospel of Matthew.
*Optional:* You may want to choose an appropriate song to begin or end the prayer.

### Gather

Gather the children in the Bible corner. Distribute the prayer handouts. Briefly rehearse the prayer responses, noting that each one is different because each is directed to a different member of the Holy Trinity.

### Pray

Begin with the Sign of the Cross as indicated. Introduce the reading with the words given, or in your own words.
(An activity for the Baptism of Jesus can be found on page 83 of *The Catholic Children's Bible Leader Guide*.)

## Closing Prayer

This prayer continues in the spirit of the activity offered for the Baptism of Jesus. However, if you did not offer this activity, you can adapt the introduction to summarize the main points of the lesson.

### Gather

Gather the children in the Bible corner and ask them to sit down. Explain that this closing prayer is a time of quiet prayer and will end with a blessing prayer.

### Pray

Follow the directions for the leader given on the prayer handout.
*Optional:* You may want to end with the song you chose for the opening prayer.

# Activity for the Baptism of Jesus

## Preparing the Way

**Scripture Focus:** Matthew 3:13–17 (Featured Story "Jesus Obeys His Heavenly Father"). The children celebrate the Baptism of Jesus by making a desert scene. John the Baptist lived in the desert before he came forward to preach, and Jesus spent forty days in the desert before his Baptism by John.

**Gather the following items:** shoebox lids, one for each child; a bag of play sand; a bag of small stones; jar lids, one for each child; a pitcher of water; a cactus or aloe plant; small paper plates, one for each child; a tray of fruit slices with a large bowl of honey for dip, enough for each child to have a slice of fruit and a plate of dip; and small plastic bags, one for each child

**Let's Look It Up!** Have the children open *The Catholic Children's Bible* to the Gospel of Matthew in the New Testament. Direct them to find chapter 3, verses 13–17. Explain that this passage recounts the Baptism of Jesus in the Jordan River by John the Baptist. Remind the children that John the Baptist lived and prayed in the desert before he began preaching, and that Jesus just spent forty days in the desert, praying and getting ready for his mission of salvation. (*Note:* Consider making the Featured Story "Jesus Obeys His Heavenly Father" the basis for your lesson.)

## Activity

1. Explain that today we will be making a miniature desert. Because the desert is so sparse and not distracting, it makes a good place for prayer. Both John the Baptist and Jesus spent time in the desert because it helped them to pray. Our miniature deserts will help us to pray.

2. Give each child a shoebox lid to use as a tray. Put on each tray, separately and in the following order, a small pile of sand, some stones, and a jar lid filled with water. Also set out a cactus or aloe plant to be passed around among the children. As you distribute each material, explain it (see bullet list) and use it as a Scripture meditation with the citations given. (You may want to write the citations on the board and challenge volunteers to find them in *The Catholic Children's Bible*.)

   - *Sand:* Suggest that the children feel how dry the sand is. Explain that the desert does not get much rain, so it is often dry and hot. After you distribute the sand, ask the children to repeat after you in prayer: "O God, . . . / like a dry, worn-out, and waterless land, / my soul is thirsty for you" (Psalm 63:1).

■ *A jar lid filled with water:* Distribute the jar lids and fill each with water. As you pour the water, suggest that the children dip their fingers carefully into it. Explain that there are some water holes in the desert, and animals come to drink at them. After you have distributed the lids and water, ask the children to repeat after you, "As a deer longs for a stream of cool water, / so I long for you, O God" (Psalm 42:1).

■ *Stones:* As you give a few stones to each child, ask them to arrange the stones in their desert scene. Explain that the desert is full of stones. Remind the children that when Jesus went to the desert to pray and to fast, the devil met him there and tempted him. Satan told Jesus to turn some of the stones into bread! Jesus said no. Jesus told Satan (and this can be the prayer to repeat), "Human beings cannot live on bread alone, but need every word that God speaks" (Matthew 4:4).

■ *Cactus or aloe plant:* You will need just one. The children can come up and carefully feel it (watch the needles!), or you can carry it to each child. Desert plants store water in their leaves, so they can have water even if it doesn't rain. Ask the children to feel the thick leaves and bodies of the cactus or aloe. Ask the children to repeat after you: "Like plants filled with water, fill us with your Holy Spirit, O Lord!"

■ *Fruit and honey:* Pass around a tray of fruit slices with a large bowl of honey dip. Be sure to arrange a substitute, like jelly, for those allergic to honey. (You may also distribute small paper plates so children can spoon out some honey.) Encourage the children to try a slice of fruit with honey. Not much food can grow in the desert, but bees live there and make honey, which John the Baptist found and ate. Honey is very nourishing and also very sweet. Ask the children to repeat after you: "O Lord, your commandments are sweeter than the purest honey!" (see Psalm 19:10).

Give the children time to look at their desert scenes and to imagine themselves in the desert. Ask them to be very still for a moment and to make up their own prayers to God.

3. At the end of the session, have the children pour the water from their jar lids back into the pitcher. To arrange for taking the desert scenes home, give each child a small plastic sandwich bag in which to carry the sand, the lid, and the stones.

# Prayers for Ordinary Time

**Scripture Focus:** Luke 10:25–37 (Featured Story "The Good Samaritan")

## Opening Prayer

**Leader:** Let us begin our prayer with the Sign of the Cross.
**All:** In the name of the Father . . .
**Leader:** In this Gospel, Jesus tells us the story of the Good Samaritan. The Samaritan was good because he helped someone in need.
**Reader:** A reading from the holy Gospel according to Luke.
*Reader then reads the Scripture passage above from* The Catholic Children's Bible.
**Leader:** Let us pray that we can all be Good Samaritans! Our response is, "Help us to be Good Samaritans, O Lord."
**All:** Help us to be Good Samaritans, O Lord.
**Leader:** When we are tempted to use mean words against others . . .
**All:** Help us to be Good Samaritans, O Lord.
**Leader:** When we are tempted to leave others out . . .
**All:** Help us to be Good Samaritans, O Lord.
**Leader:** When we are tempted to bully others just because we can . . .
**All:** Help us to be Good Samaritans, O Lord.
**Leader:** When we are inspired to help someone who needs our help . . .
**All:** Help us to be Good Samaritans, O Lord.
**Leader:** When we are inspired to give something away to someone who needs it more than we do . . .
**All:** Help us to be Good Samaritans, O Lord.
**Leader:** When we are inspired to pray for all those who are hurting or in need . . .
**All:** Help us to be Good Samaritans, O Lord.

## Closing Prayer

**Leader:** Today we learned that loving God, ourselves, and others is the meaning of the Gospel. Let us pray to live the Gospel each and every day:

Lord Jesus,
Thank you for telling us the story of the Good Samaritan. Help us to be Good Samaritans in our families, our schools, and with our friends and neighbors. Thank you, Lord Jesus, for showing us the way. Amen.

Document #: TX003063

# Ritual Guide

## Opening Prayer

### Preparation

Choose several readers to take turns reading this Gospel passage. You may want to take the part of Jesus in verses 10 through 36, the story of the Good Samaritan.
*Optional:* You may want to choose an appropriate song to begin or end the prayer.

### Gather

Gather the children in the Bible corner. Distribute the prayer handouts. Briefly rehearse the prayer response, noting that we will be hearing more about what it means to be a Good Samaritan in the Gospel reading.

### Pray

Begin with the Sign of the Cross as indicated. Introduce the reading with the words given, or in your own words. At the close of this prayer, collect the handouts and set them aside for the closing prayer.
(An activity for Ordinary Time, featuring the Parable of the Good Samaritan, can be found on page 87 of *The Catholic Children's Bible Leader Guide.*)

## Closing Prayer

### Preparation

This closing prayer is based on the Parable of the Good Samaritan.

### Gather

Gather the children in the Bible corner and distribute the handouts. Explain that in this prayer we ask Jesus to help us to do good to others, to be Good Samaritans, each and every day.

### Pray

Invite the children to pray the prayer together.
*Optional:* You may want to end with the song you chose for the opening prayer.

# Activity for Ordinary Time

## Concentrating on Love

**Scripture Focus:** Luke 10:25–37 (Featured Story "The Good Samaritan"). The children will uncover Jesus' message about showing love for God, our neighbor, and ourselves.

**Gather the following items:** thirty blank index cards; thirty index cards with the words from Luke 10:27, one word on each card; card chart; crayons or markers; and drawing paper

**Let's Look It Up!** After the game for this activity is played, you may want to have the children open *The Catholic Children's Bible* to the Gospel of Luke in the New Testament. Direct them to find chapter 10, verses 25–37. Explain that this Gospel story is the Parable of the Good Samaritan. Jesus told this story to teach us about loving God, ourselves, and our neighbor. (*Note:* Consider making the Featured Story "The Good Samaritan" the basis for your lesson.)

## Activity

1. Invite the children to play a concentration / matching game. Before class, prepare word cards that contain the words from the Scripture passage, "'Love the Lord your God with all your heart, with all your soul, with all your strength, and with all your mind'; and 'Love your neighbor as you love yourself'" (Luke 10:27). Have one word written on each card to make thirty word cards in all. Place these cards facedown in correct word order in a card chart or on the surface of a desk or table. The message should stay hidden from the children's view until they begin to make matches.

2. Distribute two blank index cards and some crayons or markers to each child. Depending on the size of the class, you may need to give one card to every child and then pair up the remaining children to work together. Invite the children to draw the same design, shape, or picture on two cards (geometric shapes, faces, nature, etc.).

3. When the children have finished their designs, collect the picture cards. Shuffle the cards to mix up the order. Then ask the children to help you put the cards in the chart or on the flat surface. Invite them to place the cards at random, picture side down, over the hidden message cards already in the chart. After all the cards have been placed, invite the children, one at a time, to pick two picture cards (top cards).

If the cards match, that child may reveal the words under those cards. If the cards do not match, the child places them back as originally found.

4. After all the matches have been found, invite the class to read together the message that has been uncovered. At this time you may direct the children to refer to their Bible and read the entire Gospel passage.

(*Note:* You may use the picture cards again to hide a different Scripture message in another lesson.)

# Prayers for Lent

**Scripture Focus:** Luke 15:11–32 (Featured Story "The Forgiving Father")

## Opening Prayer

**Leader:** Let us begin our prayer with the Sign of the Cross.

**All:** In the name of the Father . . .

**Leader:** In this Gospel, Jesus tells us the Parable of the Forgiving Father. The father had a son who ran away and spent all his money. When he had nothing left, he came back to his father and said: "I'm sorry. Please forgive me."

**Reader:** A reading from the holy Gospel according to Luke.

*Reader then reads the Scripture passage above from* The Catholic Children's Bible.

**Leader:** Sometimes we have to say "I'm sorry" to God our Father. We can say: "I'm sorry, Father. Please forgive me."

**All:** "I'm sorry, Father. Please forgive me."

**Leader:** When we have made bad choices and done wrong, we can say:

**All:** "I'm sorry, Father. Please forgive me."

**Leader:** When we have disobeyed parents, grandparents, or others in charge of us, we can say:

**All:** "I'm sorry, Father. Please forgive me."

**Leader:** When we have hurt friends with unkind words or actions, we can say:

**All:** "I'm sorry, Father. Please forgive me."

**Leader:** At one time or another, we are all like the son. We all make bad choices and need forgiveness. God our Father is always waiting for us, hoping we will return and ask forgiveness, especially in the Sacrament of Penance and Reconciliation. After we are forgiven, we have every reason to celebrate!

## Closing Prayer

**Leader:** Today we heard the story of the Forgiving Father. When the son asked forgiveness, the father forgave him. This is what God our Father is like. And when we forgive others, we are being just like God! Let us pray the prayer to God our Father that Jesus taught us:

**All:** Our Father, who art in heaven, hallowed be thy name.

Thy kingdom come, thy will be done on earth as it is in heaven.

Give us this day our daily bread, and forgive us our trespasses as we forgive those who trespass against us. And lead us not into temptation. But deliver us from evil.

Amen.

# Ritual Guide

## Opening Prayer

### Preparation

Choose one or two readers to read the short passage from this parable, or choose several readers (including yourself) to read the entire story, Luke 15:11–32. Or, choose volunteers to be the Father, the Son, and the Older Son. Instruct them to act out the story as you read it.
*Optional:* You may want to choose an appropriate song to begin or end the prayer.

### Gather

Gather the children in the Bible corner. Distribute the prayer handouts. Briefly rehearse the prayer response. Ask the children to listen for the part of the Gospel story in which the son says similar words to his father.

### Pray

Begin with the Sign of the Cross as indicated. Introduce the reading with the words given, or in your own words.
(An activity for Lent can be found on page 91 of *The Catholic Children's Bible Leader Guide.*)

## Closing Prayer

### Preparation

This prayer is based on the Parable of the Forgiving Father, and includes the Lord's Prayer, the prayer Jesus taught us.

### Gather

Gather the children in the Bible corner. Explain that the closing prayer is the Lord's Prayer, the prayer that Jesus taught us. In this prayer we ask God our Father to forgive us, and we promise to forgive others.

### Pray

Lead the children in prayer.
*Optional:* You may want to end with the song you chose for the opening prayer.

Document #: TX003065

# Activity for Lent

## Flipping for Lent

**Scripture Focus:** Luke 15:20–24 (Featured Story "The Forgiving Father"). The children will choose ways to live and grow in their Catholic faith during Lent.

**Gather the following items:** one square sheet of white paper for each child (the larger the square, the larger the flip game), and a pencil or marker for each child (*Note:* The paper must be exactly square for this game to work.)

**Let's Look It Up!** Have the children open *The Catholic Children's Bible* to the Gospel of Luke in the New Testament. Direct them to find chapter 15, verses 20–24. Explain that this passage is part of the Parable of the Lost Son—being sorry and choosing to change to be better. (*Note:* Consider making the Featured Story "The Forgiving Father" the basis for your lesson.)

## Activity

1. Gather the children for a brainstorming session. Ask, How can we live our faith and grow closer to Jesus during Lent? What special something can we do for someone else?

2. Distribute a square sheet of paper to each child. As you demonstrate the following folds, ask the children to do the same with their squares of paper: Placing the square on the desk, fold the paper by taking the two corners that are closest and joining the pointed corners in the center of the square. Explain that pressing down the fold will make a tight fold. Do the same with the other two corners.

3. Now have the children turn the paper over so that the folds are face down on their desks. Instruct them to take each pointed corner and make a tight fold toward the center of the square. The children should have a perfect square. Keeping the folds facing them, instruct the children to fold the square in half so there are two open flaps facing up. Now have them turn the folded paper over to see the other two open flaps.

4. On the top flaps, ask the children to write words associated with Lent (for example: Lent, forty, Jesus, cross). For the flip game, they choose a word and spell it as they move their fingers for each letter. Inside the top flaps, the children write numbers 1 through 8. In the game, they will choose a number and move their fingers for that amount.

5. Direct the children to refer to the list of ideas gathered at the brainstorming session. Have them choose eight different ways they want to live and grow in their faith during Lent. Instruct them to write these ideas on the eight inside hidden triangle flaps.

6. Demonstrate the finger-flip game. Have the children place their pointer fingers in the two front flaps and their thumbs in the two back flaps. Direct them to move their fingers together to close the paper square completely. Show them how to stretch their thumbs and pointer fingers at the same time to open and close the folded game. Then, moving their fingers and keeping a tight hold inside the flaps, tell them to gently pull their hands apart to open the folded game in the other direction. (Allow the children to get familiar with these movements and to be careful not to tear the paper.) After the children spell a word on the top flap and count a number from the inside flap, ask them to choose another number and lift the flap to reveal the activity they will do for that week of Lent. Encourage the children to use this game each week (or daily) during Lent as a reminder of their choices to live and grow in their faith.

# Prayers for the Annunciation of Mary

**Scripture Focus:** Luke 1:26–38 (Featured Story "Mary Trusts God Completely")

## Opening Prayer

**Leader:** Let us begin our prayer with the Sign of the Cross.

**All:** In the name of the Father . . .

**Leader:** In this Gospel passage, we learn that an angel was sent to Mary to give her a very special message. Mary was going to be the mother of God's Son, and she was to name him Jesus!

**Reader:** A reading from the holy Gospel according to Luke.

*Reader then reads the Scripture passage above from* The Catholic Children's Bible.

**Leader:** Mary said yes to God, and she can help us when we pray, "Mary, help us to say yes to God."

**All:** Mary, help us to say yes to God.

**Leader:** Saying yes to God means following Jesus and keeping on the right path, no matter what.

**All:** Mary, help us to say yes to God.

**Leader:** Sometimes life is hard. Sometimes we have problems at home, or we have a hard time in school. During hard times, it is more important than ever to follow Jesus and stay on the right path. It is also important to share our problems with our parents or another trusted adult.

**All:** Mary, help us to say yes to God.

**Leader:** Sometimes life brings wonderful surprises. We go on a family vacation, or grandparents come for a visit, or we celebrate a birthday. During happy times, we follow Jesus and stay on the right path.

**All:** Mary, help us to say yes to God.

**Leader:** Each and every day, in each and every way,

**All:** Mary, help us to say yes to God.

## Closing Prayer

**Leader:** We are happy today, because we share in Mary's happiness at being chosen to be the Mother of God. Let us pray the prayer that especially honors Mary and asks her help:

**All:** Hail Mary, full of grace, the Lord is with you.

Blessed are you among women, and blessed is the fruit of your womb, Jesus.

Holy Mary, Mother of God, pray for us sinners,

Now, and at the hour of our death.

Amen.

# Ritual Guide

## Opening Prayer

### Preparation

Choose a reader to read the passage from the Gospel of Luke.
*Optional:* You may want to choose an appropriate song to begin or end the prayer.

### Gather

Gather the children in the Bible corner. Distribute the prayer handouts. Briefly rehearse the prayer response.

### Pray

Begin with the Sign of the Cross as indicated. Introduce the reading with the words given, or in your own words. At the close of the prayer, collect the prayer handouts. Set them aside for the closing prayer (if the children do not yet know the Hail Mary by heart).
(An activity for the Annunciation of Mary can be found on page 95 of *The Catholic Children's Bible Leader Guide.*)

## Closing Prayer

This ancient prayer is based on the angel's words to Mary at the Annunciation.

### Gather

Gather the children in the Bible corner. Explain that the closing prayer is a well-known prayer to Mary. Encourage those who know it by heart to set aside their papers. (Allow those who do not yet know this prayer to take the prayer handouts home. Remind them to ask their families for help in learning this prayer.)

### Pray

Lead the children in prayer.
*Optional:* You may want to end with the song you chose for the opening prayer.

# Activity for the Annunciation of Mary

## Message Received!

**Scripture Focus:** Luke 1:26–30 (Featured Story "Mary Trusts God Completely"). The children recognize the importance of angels, God's messengers.

**Gather the following items:** statue of Mary; blue and white crepe paper; tape; sheets of white construction paper, markers, scissors, and craft sticks, one of each for each child; glitter glue (optional); and several bottles of glue

**Let's Look It Up!** Have the children open *The Catholic Children's Bible* to the Gospel of Luke in the New Testament. Direct them to find chapter 1, verses 26–30. Explain that this passage is part of the announcement of the birth of Jesus. (*Note:* Consider making the Featured Story "Mary Trusts God Completely" the basis for your lesson.)

## Activity

1. Ask the children to work with you to make a Mary shrine in the room. Place a table and a statue of Mary against a wall. Provide strips of blue and white crepe paper. Help the children attach the strips to the wall above the statue, alternating by color. Then show them how to twist them together in pairs and attach the free ends to the front of the table to make a canopy over the statue. When the canopy is finished, ask the children to return to their seats.

2. Distribute a sheet of white construction paper, a marker, and a scissors to each child. Demonstrate how to fold the sheet of paper in half. Holding their fingers together, the children should place their hand on the paper (left for right-handers, right for left-handers). Stress that the thumb should be on the fold line. Instruct them to trace their handprint on the paper and to remember to keep their fingers together.

3. Have the children carefully cut out their handprints, emphasizing not to cut the folded side. Then ask the children to open up the cut-outs and flip their "angel wings" upside down so the fingertips are pointing down. If you have provided glitter glue, invite the children to use it to add some detail on the wings.

4. Distribute a craft stick to each child and make several bottles of glue available. Direct the children to glue the craft stick in the middle of the wings. The children should then draw their angel's face at the top of the craft stick. Then instruct them

to copy part of the angel's message on the stick or wings. They may choose from the following:

- "Peace be with you!"
- "The Lord is with you."
- "The Lord has greatly blessed you!" (Luke 1:28)
- "Don't be afraid, Mary."
- "God has been gracious to you." (Luke 1:30)

5. Invite the children to hold their angels and process to the Mary shrine. Have the children sing a hymn to Mary or recite the Hail Mary as they process. When all have gathered at the statue, invite them to read the Scripture passage on their angel. Have the children bring their angels home to share God's message with their families.

# Prayers for Palm / Passion Sunday

**Scripture Focus:** Matthew 21:1–17 (Featured Story "The Crowds Praise Jesus")

## Opening Prayer

**Leader:** Let us begin our prayer with the Sign of the Cross.

**All:** In the name of the Father . . .

**Leader:** In this Gospel, we read that Jesus was welcomed by the crowds. They were so happy that he had come to them! They cried out their praises.

**Reader:** A reading from the holy Gospel according to Matthew.

*Reader then reads the Scripture passage above from* The Catholic Children's Bible.

**Leader:** We too can welcome Jesus into our hearts. We too can say: "Praise to Jesus! Praise be to God!"

**All:** Praise to Jesus! Praise be to God!

**Leader:** At every Eucharist, we praise Jesus. We thank him for coming to us. We say, "Hosanna in the highest. Blessed is he who comes in the name of the Lord. Hosanna in the highest" *(Roman Missal)*.

**All:** Praise to Jesus! Praise be to God!

**Leader:** At every Eucharist, we praise Jesus. We pray to the Father in Jesus, with Jesus, and through Jesus. In every Eucharist, we become one with Jesus.

**All:** Praise to Jesus! Praise be to God!

**Leader:** At every Eucharist, Jesus enters into our hearts. We pray, "Lord, I am not worthy that you should enter under my roof" *(Roman Missal)*. We pray for healing.

**All:** Praise to Jesus! Praise be to God!

**Leader:** Thank you, Jesus, for coming to Jerusalem. Thank you for coming to us in every Eucharist.

**All:** Praise to Jesus! Praise be to God!

## Closing Prayer

**Leader:** Today we gave praise and honor to Jesus. We promised to honor him all during Holy Week. Let us offer this prayer of praise from the Mass, as we pray with the whole Church.

**All:**

Holy, holy, holy Lord God of hosts.
Heaven and earth are full of your glory.
Hosanna in the highest.
Blessed is he who comes in the name of the Lord.
Hosanna in the highest.

*(Roman Missal)*

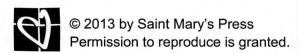

# Ritual Guide

## Opening Prayer

### Preparation

Choose a reader or several readers to read the passage from the Gospel of Matthew.
*Optional:* You may want to choose an appropriate song to begin or end the prayer.

### Gather

Gather the children in the Bible corner. Distribute the prayer handouts. Briefly rehearse the prayer response. Explain to the children that the word *Hosanna,* which they may hear or have heard today, means "Praise!"

### Pray

Begin with the Sign of the Cross as indicated. Introduce the prayer with the words given, or in your own words. At the close of this prayer, collect the prayer handouts and set them aside for the closing prayer. (An activity for Palm / Passion Sunday can be found on page 99 of *The Catholic Children's Bible Leader Guide.*)

## Closing Prayer

### Preparation

This prayer is an acclamation found at the end of the Preface at every Eucharist. It directly quotes the words of the crowds in Jerusalem as they greeted Jesus.

### Gather

Gather the children in the Bible corner. Explain that the closing prayer is a prayer of praise that we say at every Eucharist. The word *Hosanna* means "Praise!"

### Pray

Invite the children to pray the prayer together, or to repeat each line after you.
*Optional:* You may want to end with the song you chose for the opening prayer.

Document #: TX003067

# Activity for Palm / Passion Sunday

## We Honor Jesus

**Scripture Focus:** Matthew 21:1–11 (Featured Story "The Crowds Praise Jesus"). The children decide ways to honor Jesus, make their own palm branches with these ideas written on them, and then carry the branches in procession to the Bible corner.

**Gather the following items:** large sheets of green construction paper with a large "palm frond" drawn on each, black or brown markers, and scissors, one of each for each child. (To draw the "palm frond," fold the green paper in half the long way. With the fold at the bottom, draw a curved line from the left-hand edge at the fold, up to the open end, and down to the right-hand edge of the fold. Go over the line with a dark marker so that children can cut around it. When open, this will look like a broad leaf.)

**Let's Look It Up!** Have the children open *The Catholic Children's Bible* to the Gospel of Matthew in the New Testament. Direct them to find chapter 21, verses 1–11. (*Note:* Consider making the Featured Story "The Crowds Praise Jesus" the basis for your lesson.)

## Activity

1. Explain to the children that all the people were happy to see Jesus. Even the children were waving palm branches to honor him. Today is the beginning of Holy Week. We will make special palm branches on which we can write the ways we will honor Jesus during this special Holy Week that we celebrate in the coming days.

2. Distribute the green paper with the palms drawn on them, one to each child, along with a pair of scissors. Instruct the children to cut along the line, and open their palm fronds.

3. Distribute the markers and instruct the children to write their names in big letters on one side of the palm.

4. Explain that on the other side of the palm, each child will write one way to honor Jesus in this coming week. Brainstorm ideas using the following suggestions if needed: saying bedtime prayers, helping at home, listening better in school, helping classmates. Ask the children to choose one of these ideas, or think of one on their own, and to write it on the other side of the palm.

5. Gather the children in one corner of the room, in the hallway, or in another convenient spot. Ask them to hold their palms high and wave them slowly while

everyone processes to the Bible corner. Choose an appropriate song to play or sing to honor Jesus, preferably one that includes the word *Hosanna*! When the song begins, lead the children, in a roundabout way, to the Bible corner. When the song stops, and with the children gathered in the Bible corner, ask each one to read aloud his or her way of honoring Jesus this week, and then to leave the palm on or around the Bible. At the close of the session, give the palms back to the children to take home.

# Prayers for the Triduum

**Scripture Focus:** Mark 14:22–24, Holy Thursday; Matthew 27:50–54, Good Friday; Matthew 28:5–9, Easter Sunday (Featured Stories: "The Last Supper," "Jesus Gives His Life for Us," "Jesus Wants Us to Help Others Know Him")

## Opening Prayer

**Leader:** Let us begin our prayer with the Sign of the Cross.

**All:** In the name of the Father . . .

**Leader:** The readings for the holiest days of the year, the Three Days when we participate in Jesus' Last Supper, his death on the cross, and his Resurrection, help us to remember all that Jesus did for us.

**Reader:** A reading from the holy Gospel according to _____.

*(Reader then reads one of the Scripture passages noted above from* The Catholic Children's Bible.*)*

**Leader:** Jesus is our Savior, and he has set us free. Let us pray: "Save us, Savior of the world, for by your Cross and Resurrection, you have set us free" *(Roman Missal).*

**All:** Save us, Savior of the world, for by your Cross and Resurrection, you have set us free.

**Leader:** Jesus, at your Last Supper, you gave us the gift of the Eucharist. Help us to stay close to you always.

**All:** Save us, Savior of the world, for by your Cross and Resurrection, you have set us free.

**Leader:** Jesus, at your death on the cross, you gave your life for us, your friends. Help us to live our lives as your true friends.

**All:** Save us, Savior of the world, for by your Cross and Resurrection, you have set us free.

**Leader:** Jesus, on Easter Sunday you rose from the dead to bring us your new life. Help us to follow you from death to life.

**All:** Save us, Savior of the world, for by your Cross and Resurrection, you have set us free.

## Closing Prayer

**Leader:** When we celebrate the Three Days, we are with Jesus in a special way—at the Last Supper, at his death on the cross, and in his Resurrection from the dead. Let us thank him for all his gifts to us. Please repeat each line after me. [The lines end at the slash marks.]

> You give us the Bread of Life. / We thank you! /
> You give us the cross of death. / We thank you! /
> You give us your Risen Life. / We thank you! /
> In your death and in your life, / we are yours, Lord Jesus. /
> In your death and in your life, / we are yours. /
> Amen.

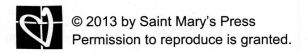

# Ritual Guide

## Opening Prayer

### Preparation

Choose a reader to read one of the three passages given for the Triduum. (These Triduum references are not from the *Lectionary* but are parallel passages from the Featured Stories.)
*Optional:* You may want to choose an appropriate song to begin or end the prayer. (Suggestion: "Were You There When They Crucified My Lord?")

### Gather

Gather the children in the Bible corner. Distribute the prayer handouts. Briefly rehearse the prayer response. If preferred, the response can be shortened to, "Save us, Savior of the world."

### Pray

Begin with the Sign of the Cross as indicated. Introduce the reading with the words given for the Leader, or in your own words. Collect the prayer handouts. As the closing prayer is a repetitive prayer, the children will not need them again.
(An activity for the Triduum can be found on page 103 of *The Catholic Children's Bible Leader Guide*.)

## Closing Prayer

### Preparation

This prayer refers to each of the events of the Triduum: the Last Supper, Jesus' death on the cross, and his Resurrection at Easter.

### Gather

Gather the children in the Bible corner. Explain that our closing prayer is a prayer thanking Jesus for giving us himself in the Eucharist, for dying on the cross for us, and for giving us new life at Easter. Tell the children that you will be the leader and that they should repeat each line after you.

### Pray

Lead the children in prayer.
*Optional:* You may want to end with the song you chose for the opening prayer, or with a song of Resurrection.

# Activity for the Triduum (Holy Thursday, Good Friday, Easter Sunday)

## We Celebrate the Three Days

**Scripture Focus:** Holy Thursday (the Last Supper): Mark 14:22–24 (Featured Story "The Last Supper"); Good Friday: Matthew 27:50–54 (Featured Story "Jesus Gives His Life for Us"); Easter Sunday: Matthew 28:5–9 (Featured Story "Jesus Wants Us to Help Others Know Him"). The children make a mobile with representative symbols—a Host and chalice, a cross, and a "rising sun"—of each of the Three Days of the Triduum, with a prayer to Jesus on each symbol.

**Gather the following items:** wire coat hangers, one for each child; brown, gold, and white construction paper from which to cut the symbols; scissors; several bottles of glue; thread or string; and a needle or hole punch for making holes in paper (To make the symbols, you might want to start by making a template for each out of cardboard and then trace around it as many times as needed for the number of children in your class. Draw a simple chalice with a "rounded" shape for the top and a broad "leg" for the bottom, all in one piece. Trace this onto gold construction paper. To make the Host, cut out a circle of an appropriate size that will fit on the paper chalice. Trace this onto white construction paper. Cut out a cross, being careful not to make it too thin. Trace this onto brown construction paper. Cut out a circle for the sun, also including "rays" coming out of it. Trace this onto gold construction paper.)

**Let's Look It Up!** Have the children open *The Catholic Children's Bible* to the New Testament. Direct them to find the illustrations for each of the Featured Stories listed in the "Scripture Focus" section, so that they are made aware of the entire three days of the Triduum. (*Note:* Consider making these Featured Stories the basis for your lesson.)

## Activity

1. Explain to the children that the Church celebrates three special days during Holy Week. These days are called the Triduum, which means "three days." (The Triduum days begin at sunset, so the Triduum lasts from Holy Thursday evening through Easter Sunday evening.) These are the days that Jesus gave us the gift of the Eucharist at the Last Supper, and then suffered, died, and rose again for us. These are the most solemn and serious days of the entire year.

2. Share the following with the children:

> ➤ To celebrate these days, and to remind us of what they mean, we will make a mobile. On it we will hang three special symbols of Jesus' gifts to us. One symbol is the Host and chalice, for the Holy Eucharist, the gift Jesus gave us on Holy Thursday. Another symbol is the cross, for Jesus' death on Good Friday. The third symbol is the shining sun, for Jesus' Resurrection on Easter Sunday.

3. Distribute the paper chalices and Hosts, along with scissors and glue, and ask the children to cut out the symbols. Then instruct them to glue the bottom of the paper Host to the top of the chalice.

4. Distribute the paper crosses and ask the children to cut them out.

5. Distribute the paper suns and ask the children to cut them out.

6. Ask the children to turn the chalice over and write a message to Jesus on the back of it. (Suggestions: *Thank you, Jesus, for Holy Communion*; *Jesus, thank you for being with us always*; *Jesus, I love you.*)

7. Ask the children to turn the cross over and write a message to Jesus on the back: (Suggestions: *Thank you, Jesus, for all you did for us*; *Jesus, I love you.*)

8. Ask the children to turn the sun over and write a message to Jesus on the back: (Suggestions: *Alleluia! Jesus is risen!*; *Risen Jesus, I love you*; *Thank you, Jesus, for new life!*)

9. Using the needle or hole punch, poke holes in the symbols as follows: at the top of the Host, at the top of the cross, and at the end of one of the rays of the sun.

10. Distribute three pieces of thread or string, of varying lengths, to each child. (Holes made by needles will need thread; holes made with a hole punch will need string.) Help the children attach the string to the symbols.

11. Distribute the wire hangers. Help the children hang the symbols from the wire hangers.

12. Review the meaning of the symbols by asking volunteers to tell the "story" of the symbol. Remind the children to tell the story at home when showing their mobiles to their families.

# Prayers for the Easter Season

**Scripture Focus:** John 10:11–16 (Featured Story "Jesus Is the Good Shepherd")

## Opening Prayer

**Leader:** Let us begin our prayer with the Sign of the Cross.

**All:** In the name of the Father . . .

**Leader:** Jesus is our Good Shepherd, who died and rose for us. He knows his sheep, and we know him. He calls us by name.

**Reader:** A reading from the Gospel according to John.

*Reader then reads the Scripture passage above from* The Catholic Children's Bible.

**Leader:** We want to listen to Jesus and follow him. Let us respond in prayer: "We will listen and follow. Alleluia!"

**All:** We will listen and follow. Alleluia!

**Leader:** When we face choices to do good or to do wrong, help us, Good Shepherd, and call us by name.

**All:** We will listen and follow. Alleluia!

**Leader:** When we feel alone and are looking for a friend, help us, Good Shepherd, and call us by name.

**All:** We will listen and follow. Alleluia!

**Leader:** When we are concerned for others who are sick or in need, help us, Good Shepherd, and call us by name.

**All:** We will listen and follow. Alleluia!

## Closing Prayer

**Leader:** Today we learned that Jesus is the Good Shepherd who cares for us, his sheep. Let us pray to him, who died and rose for us:

**All:** Good Shepherd, you know us and love us.

Help us to stay close to you always.

Help us to listen to your voice and follow wherever you lead us.

We ask this in your name, Good Shepherd.

Amen.

Document #: TX003069

# Ritual Guide

## Opening Prayer

### Preparation

Choose a reader to read the passage from the Gospel of John.
*Optional:* You may want to choose an appropriate song to begin or end the prayer.

### Gather

Gather the children in the Bible corner. Distribute the prayer handouts. Briefly rehearse the prayer response. Remind the children that Alleluia means "Praise God" and is a special Easter acclamation of praise.

### Pray

Begin with the Sign of the Cross as indicated. Introduce the reading with the words given, or in your own words. Collect the handouts and set them aside for the Closing Prayer.
(An activity for the Easter season can be found on page 107 of *The Catholic Children's Bible Leader Guide.*)

## Closing Prayer

### Preparation

Gather the children in the Bible corner. Explain that this closing prayer asks Jesus, our Good Shepherd, to take care of us and to help us follow him.

### Pray

Lead the children in prayer. You may ask the group to pray all together or to repeat each line after you.
*Optional:* You may want to end with the song you chose for the opening prayer.

Document #: TX003069

# Activity for the Easter Season

## The Good Shepherd

**Scripture Focus:** John 10:11–16 (Featured Story "Jesus Is the Good Shepherd"). The children play a game based on the Scripture passage, and then they make sheep with marshmallows. (*Optional:* If you have access to a kitchen, you can make s'mores with the children.)

**Gather the following items:** a picture of Jesus as the Good Shepherd; a stuffed sheep; one or two bags of both large and small marshmallows; toothpicks, several for each child; and if making s'mores, graham crackers and chocolate bars, as needed

**Let's Look It Up!** Have the children open *The Catholic Children's Bible* to the Gospel of John in the New Testament. Direct them to find chapter 10, verses 11–16. (*Note:* Consider making the Featured Story "Jesus Is the Good Shepherd" the basis for your lesson.)

## Activity

1. Explain that the passage from Scripture today tells us that Jesus is the Shepherd who died and rose for us, his sheep. Jesus wants us to be with him, now and forever, as part of his flock.

2. Explain that Jesus is the Good Shepherd. Show the picture of Jesus as the Good Shepherd. Explain that shepherds care for sheep and defend them from wolves and thieves. Explain that in some parts of the world, people are still shepherds.

3. Bring out the stuffed sheep. Ask for a volunteer to be the wolf. Ask one or two children to close their eyes, and instruct the wolf to snatch the sheep and then hide it somewhere in the room. Then have the children who closed their eyes look for the sheep while the rest of the group calls out "hot," "cold," or "warm," depending on how close the seekers come to finding the sheep. Repeat this game until all the children have had a chance to look for the stolen sheep.

4. When the game is over, hand out the marshmallows and toothpicks and have each child make her or his own sheep. If you have access to a kitchen, consider making s'mores for a treat. Explain that the graham cracker is the field, the chocolate is the ground, and the marshmallow is the sheep.

# Prayers for Pentecost

**Scripture Focus:** Galatians 5:22–23

## Opening Prayer

**Leader:** Let us begin with the Sign of the Cross.
**All:** In the name of the Father . . .
**Leader:** We receive the gift of the Holy Spirit in Baptism and Confirmation. Let us listen to hear all the good gifts we are given as we follow the leading of the Holy Spirit.
**Reader:** A reading from the Letter of Paul to the Galatians.
*Reader then reads the Scripture passage above from* The Catholic Children's Bible.
**Leader:** Let us thank the Holy Spirit for all of his good gifts and fruits as we pray:
"Thank you, Holy Spirit."
**All:** Thank you, Holy Spirit.
**Leader:** For your fruits of love, joy, and peace,
**All:** Thank you, Holy Spirit.
**Leader:** For your fruits of patience, kindness, and goodness,
**All:** Thank you, Holy Spirit.
**Leader:** For your fruits of faithfulness and humility,
**All:** Thank you, Holy Spirit.
**Leader:** For your fruit of self-control,
**All:** Thank you, Holy Spirit.

## Closing Prayer

**Leader:** Today we celebrated the coming of the Holy Spirit to the Apostles, and to us in Baptism and Confirmation. We each received a special fruit of the Holy Spirit. Let us close with a prayer to the Holy Spirit:
**All:** Come, Holy Spirit, fill our hearts with your love. Help us to share the fruits of the Spirit with all we meet. We ask this *(make the Sign of the Cross)* in the name of the Father, and of the Son, and of the Holy Spirit. Amen.

Document #: TX003070

# Ritual Guide

## Opening Prayer

### Preparation

Choose a reader to read the passage from Saint Paul's Letter to the Galatians.
*Optional:* You may want to choose an appropriate song to begin or end the prayer.

### Gather

Gather the children in the Bible corner. Distribute the prayer handouts. Briefly rehearse the prayer response. Remind the children that they received the Holy Spirit in Baptism, and, if they follow Jesus, the fruits of the Holy Spirit will be seen in their actions.

### Pray

Begin with the Sign of the Cross as indicated. Introduce the prayer with the words given, or in your own words. Collect the handouts and set them aside for the closing prayer.
(An activity for Pentecost can be found on page 111 of *The Catholic Children's Bible Leader Guide.*)

## Closing Prayer

This prayer is based on and integrated into the activity offered for Pentecost. However, the introduction and prayer can be adapted to summarize the main point of any session about the Holy Spirit.

### Gather

Gather the children in the Bible corner. Explain that in the closing prayer, we are asking the Holy Spirit to come to each of us and to help us share his fruits of love, peace, and joy, and all the other fruits he gives us.

### Pray

Lead the children in prayer.
*Optional:* You may want to end with the song you chose for the opening prayer.

# Activity for Pentecost

## Come, Holy Spirit!

**Scripture Focus:** Galatians 5:22–23. The children review the coming of the Holy Spirit at Pentecost, and also in the Sacraments of Baptism and Confirmation. They make headbands as a reminder that the Holy Spirit is with them, and each child chooses one of the fruits of the Spirit as given in Galatians 5:22–23.

**Gather the following items:** *For the headbands:* strips of yellow construction paper, two for each child; flames cut from red construction paper, one for each child; and a stapler and scissors. *For the fruits of the Spirit:* a tray; index cards, enough for each child to have one, with one fruit of the Spirit from today's Scripture verse written on it (duplicates are fine); and a recording of a Holy Spirit song and the appropriate equipment to play it. Check sacramental records of the children in preparation for the discussion of Baptism and Confirmation.

**Let's Look It Up!** Have the children open *The Catholic Children's Bible* to the Letter to the Galatians in the New Testament. Direct them to find chapter 5, verses 22–23. Explain that today we will celebrate the coming of the Holy Spirit, each receiving a "fruit of the Spirit" as we hear in Saint Paul's Letter to the Galatians.

## Activity

1. Explain to the children that before Jesus ascended into Heaven, he promised that the Holy Spirit would come down upon the Apostles to help them spread the Good News. (*Optional:* Have the children find and read the Acts of the Apostles 2:1–4 in *The Catholic Children's Bible*.)

2. Explain that we also have received the Holy Spirit in Baptism, and the strengthening of the Holy Spirit in Confirmation. Note that most children are baptized when they are infants. Most of us are confirmed in our teen years.

3. Distribute two strips of yellow construction paper and a red flame to each child. Staple the strips together to make one long strip, adjust the strip around the child's head, cut the excess, and staple the ends together to fit. Remove the headband from the child's head and then staple the flame to the front of the headband.

4. Gather the children in the Bible corner. Ask them to sit quietly as you play a recording of a Holy Spirit song. You may also teach the participants the Taizé chant

*"Veni Sancte Spiritus"* (meaning, "Come, Holy Spirit"). The refrain can be sung as a prayer even without the verses.

5. Explain that each of us will receive one special fruit of the Holy Spirit. Pass around the tray with the index cards on it, making sure all the cards are turned over so the students cannot see what is written on them. Ask each child to take a card and to read the name of that fruit aloud. As time permits, discuss the meaning of each fruit in that child's life or experience.

6. Close with the closing prayer as given on the handout "Prayers for Pentecost" (Document #: TX003070).

# Chapter 11

## Word and Sacrament: Preparing for the Sacraments of Christian Initiation and the Sacrament of Penance and Reconciliation

Preparing children for the Sacraments of Christian Initiation is one of the great privileges and great responsibilities of the teacher or catechist. Most often, younger elementary-age children will need preparation for the Sacrament of Penance and Reconciliation and for the Eucharist. Sometimes, depending on individual circumstances, an older child will require preparation for Baptism. Again, depending on an individual situation or on local custom, preparation for the Sacrament of Confirmation is offered to elementary-aged children.

In every instance, *The Catholic Children's Bible* can be a helpful catalyst to a scriptural understanding of the Sacraments of Christian Initiation, as well as the Sacrament of Penance and Reconciliation. Used alongside basal texts specifically geared to the teaching of these Sacraments, *The Catholic Children's Bible* can introduce children to the Word of God, inculcating an understanding of that powerful Word, and thus preparing the children to hear and to meet that Word, Jesus Christ, in the Sacrament they are about to receive.

At the end of this chapter is a comprehensive list of the biblical stories and events most helpful in preparing for the Sacraments of Penance and Reconciliation, and for each of the Sacraments of Christian Initiation. What follows here are two suggested formats for introducing any of these stories and events into a session of Sacrament preparation:

- Note the Scripture story presented in your basal text, and ask the children to find the same story in *The Catholic Children's Bible*. Direct attention to the featured pages. Point out the vocabulary words, and then ask volunteers to read aloud the Featured Story. Ask the children to describe the illustrations. Then discuss the Understand It!, Live It!, and Tell It! panels. As you lead the children through the lesson as suggested by the basal text, you may find that, having been prepared to hear and understand the Scripture passage through the featured pages of *The Catholic Children's Bible,* they will more easily grasp the implications of the Scripture passage in relation to the Sacrament for which they are preparing.

- Alternatively, you may want to present the lesson offered by the basal text, and then, as a review, ask the children to open to the same story or event in *The Catholic Children's Bible.* Using the Tell It! panel on the featured pages, ask the children to take turns retelling the Scripture story. Ask one or more volunteers to read aloud the Featured Story, and use the Understand It! and Live It! panels to enhance the students' understanding of the Scripture passage. You may also want to review the vocabulary words highlighted in the quotation. This would be an appropriate time to point out again the significance of the story in relation to the particular Sacrament for which the children are preparing.

The Featured Stories from *The Catholic Children's Bible* listed in the following chart are categorized by the particular Sacraments with which they are associated in the Tradition of the Church and consequently in many basal texts.

# Baptism

| Scripture Passage | Featured Story | Page |
|---|---|---|
| Genesis 6:9—9:17 | God Saves Noah's Family (The Flood) | 34 |
| Exodus 14:5–29 | God Leads the Israelites Out of Egypt (Crossing the Red Sea) | 122 |
| Matthew 3:13–17 | Jesus Obeys His Heavenly Father (The Baptism of Jesus) | 1452 |
| Matthew 19:13–15 | Jesus Welcomes Children! (Jesus Blesses Little Children) | 1496 |
| Matthew 28:1–20 | Jesus Wants Us to Help Others Know Him (The Resurrection and the Great Commission) | 1520 |
| Mark 1:1–8 | John the Baptist Prepares People for Jesus (Preaching of John the Baptist) | 1526 |
| John 3:1–21 | We Are Born Again through Baptism | 1658 |
| John 13:1–17 | Jesus Washes the Disciples' Feet | 1686 |
| 1 Corinthians 12:12–27 | Every Baptized Person Is a Part of the Church | 1808 |
| Galatians 3:26–28 | God Loves All People Equally (Union with Jesus in Baptism) | 1836 |
| Ephesians 4:1–6 | Treat Other People with Kindness (One Faith, One Baptism) | 1846 |
| Colossians 3:12–17 | Thank God for All He Has Done for You (The New Life of the Christian) | 1866 |
| 1 John 3:11–18 | We Must Love One Another | 1936 |
| Revelation 21:1–7 | The New Jerusalem (We Are God's People) | 1968 |

# The Sacrament of Penance and Reconciliation

In the Tradition of the Church, the Sacrament of Penance and Reconciliation is considered a renewal of Baptism, when our sins are again forgiven and we are restored to our grace-filled relationship with God. Many of the passages listed in the Baptism chart can easily be introduced into catechesis for the Sacrament of Penance and Reconciliation. However, the chart for Penance and Reconciliation highlights those stories and events emphasizing the forgiveness of sins, most often cited for preparation sessions in basal texts.

| Scripture Passage | Featured Story | Page |
|---|---|---|
| Genesis 3:1–24 | Adam and Eve Disobey God | 26 |
| Exodus 19:16—20:17 | God Gives His People the Ten Commandments | 132 |
| Psalm 51 | We Ask God to Forgive Our Sins | 878 |
| Matthew 3:13–17 | Jesus Obeys His Heavenly Father (The Baptism of Jesus) | 1452 |
| Matthew 25:31–46 | We Must Care for People in Need (The Final Judgment) | 1510 |
| Mark 2:1–12 | Jesus Heals People from Sin and Sickness (Jesus Heals a Paralyzed Man) | 1530 |
| Mark 12:28–34 | Love Is the Greatest Commandment | 1556 |
| Luke 7:36–50 | Jesus Forgives a Woman's Sins | 1596 |
| Luke 10:25–37 | The Good Samaritan (The Great Commandment) | 1608 |
| Luke 15:11–32 | The Forgiving Father (The Prodigal Son) | 1620 |
| Luke 19:1–10 | Zacchaeus Wants to Meet Jesus | 1630 |
| John 14:15–31 | Jesus Sends the Holy Spirit to Help Us | 1690 |
| John 20:11–29 | The Risen Jesus Appears to Mary Magdalene (Jesus Gives the Disciples Power to Forgive Sins) | 1702 |

# The Sacrament of the Eucharist

The Eucharist is the "sum and summary of our faith" (*Catechism of the Catholic Church,* 1327) and the essential Scripture account for preparing children for this Sacrament is, of course, the account of the institution of the Eucharist at the Last Supper. However, there are many other supporting texts associated with the Eucharist. Some emphasize God's gifts to us throughout salvation history. Others specifically relate to the celebration of the Sacrament in the Holy Sacrifice of the Mass. Many accounts found in preparatory texts for First Communion are supported and enhanced by the Featured Stories in the *The Catholic Children's Bible.*

| Scripture Passage | Featured Story | Page |
|---|---|---|
| Genesis 1:1—2:3 | God Made Us to Love and to Be Loved | 22 |
| Exodus 3:1–17 | God Hears His People's Cries | 104 |
| 2 Samuel 6:12–19 | David Brings the Ark of the Lord to Jerusalem (David Dances before the Ark) | 424 |
| Matthew 6:5–13 | Jesus Teaches Us How to Pray (The Lord's Prayer) | 1460 |
| Mark 10:46–52 | Jesus Helps a Blind Man to See | 1550 |
| Mark 14:12–26 | The Last Supper | 1560 |
| Luke 4:16–22 | Jesus Says He Came to Save Us | 1586 |
| Luke 24:13–35 | Two Disciples Meet the Risen Jesus | 1644 |
| John 6:1–15 | Jesus Feeds a Huge Crowd | 1666 |
| John 13:1–17 | Jesus Washes the Disciples' Feet | 1686 |
| Acts of the Apostles 2:1–42 | The Holy Spirit Comes to the Disciples | 1714 |

# The Sacrament of Confirmation

The Sacrament of Confirmation completes Christian initiation. Although the usual Roman Catholic practice is to offer this Sacrament to adolescents, it may be helpful for some teachers and catechists preparing elementary-age children for this Sacrament to consult the following list, as it highlights the work of the Holy Spirit throughout salvation history, particularly through the symbols of water, fire, breath, and the action of anointing.

| Scripture Passage | Featured Story | Page |
|---|---|---|
| Genesis 1:1—2:3 | God Made Us to Love and to Be Loved | 22 |
| Genesis 6:9—9:17 | God Saves Noah's Family | 34 |
| Exodus 14:5–29 | God Leads the Israelites Out of Egypt | 122 |
| 1 Samuel 16:1–13 | Samuel Anoints David as the Future King | 390 |
| 1 Kings 3:4–15 | Solomon Asks God for Wisdom | 458 |
| 1 Kings 18:16–39 | Elijah Shows God's Power | 486 |
| 1 Kings 19:1–16 | God Speaks to Elijah in a Whisper | 490 |
| 2 Kings 4:8–37 | Elisha Brings a Boy Back to Life | 506 |
| Psalm 150 | We Praise God with Music and Song! | 958 |

| Passage (cont.) | Featured Story (cont.) | Page (cont.) |
|---|---|---|
| Matthew 3:13–17 | Jesus Obeys His Heavenly Father (The Baptism of Jesus) | 1452 |
| Matthew 28:1–20 | Jesus Wants Us to Help Others Know Him | 1520 |
| Mark 1:1–8 | John the Baptist Prepares People for Jesus | 1526 |
| Luke 4:16–22 | Jesus Says He Came to Save Us | 1586 |
| John 3:1–21 | We Are Born Again through Baptism (Jesus and Nicodemus) | 1658 |
| John 4:5–42 | Jesus Is the Source of Eternal Life (Jesus and the Samaritan Woman) | 1662 |
| John 14:15–31 | Jesus Sends the Holy Spirit to Help Us | 1690 |
| Acts of the Apostles 2:1–42 | The Holy Spirit Comes to the Disciples | 1714 |
| Romans 12:1–8 | God Has Given Each of Us a Gift to Share with Others | 1788 |
| 1 Corinthians 12:12–27 | Every Baptized Person Is a Part of the Church | 1808 |
| Ephesians 4:1–6 | Treat Other People with Kindness (One People, One God, One Faith) | 1846 |
| Revelation 21:1–7 | The New Jerusalem | 1968 |

# Chapter 12

## From Here to Home: Sharing Scripture with the Family

### Here to Home

The Word of God is central in the life of the Church. And, the Second Vatican Council says that family is the domestic Church (see *Dogmatic Constitution on the Church* [*Lumen Gentium,* 1965], 11). Indeed, the family is the first place from which the Word is received and the first place it is nurtured (see *National Directory for Catechesis*, 29.D).

Thus, it is important for us, as ministers of the Word, to support families and encourage their understanding of Scripture. In this chapter, we provide you with practical suggestions for helping families with children to deepen their knowledge of the Word.

Here are some ways for you to connect what you do in the classroom with what the children experience in the home.

### *Carry It Home*

Give the children a word, an image, or a question from Scripture that they can "carry" home, either tangibly or in their imaginations. A carry-home can be anything that helps the child to remember the Scripture story or the message from the Scripture story. For example, in the story "Jesus Calls People to Follow Him" (John 1:35–51), Jesus says, "Come and see" (verse 39). After discussing the story and what it is that Jesus wants us to "see," provide each child with a 3-x-5-inch card and ask them to write the words of Jesus on the card. Then ask that they take the card home and make a note (on the blank side of the card) whenever they "see" Jesus working in their lives. For instance, a child may write: "Monday at school: Jenna helped me when I didn't understand my math." Encourage the children to share their cards with their family and ask family members where they "see" Jesus.

You can design a carry-home in any way that you choose. It might simply be an image of Jesus that the students "carry home" in their imagination. For instance, you may ask them to carry home an image of Jesus as the Good Shepherd or carry home an image of Jesus feeding the five thousand.

Examples of other carry-homes include a craft, a song, a prayer from *The Catholic Children's Bible,* a question to discuss with family, and so on.

## Post It!

A post-it is a type of carry-home that you can "post" in the home. Many homes use the refrigerator as a place to post handmade works of art, family photographs, and important reminders. What better place to post the Word of God—right there alongside all the other family information. Posting easy-to-remember phrases can help children to learn the Word of God and can prompt family discussion about Scripture.

Make a simple take-home handout with a word or phrase from the Bible story you are studying. Or, you can ask children to make their own flyer, handout, or poster to be displayed on the refrigerator, on the bathroom mirror, or in the child's room.

Another idea is to make a mini take-home and have children write a word or phrase on a small piece of paper to post at home. Sometimes smaller is better.

Furthermore, you will note that *The Catholic Children's Bible* provides you with age-appropriate phrases and words that are good for posting. Here are a few examples of possible post-its from *The Catholic Children's Bible:*

- "God said, 'I am who I am.'" (Exodus 3:14)

- "Israel, remember this! The Lord—and the Lord alone—is our God. Love the Lord your God with all your heart, with all your soul, and with all your strength." (Deuteronomy 6:4)

- "Speak, Lord, your servant is listening." (1 Samuel 3:9)

- "The Lord is my shepherd; / I have everything I need." (Psalm 23:1)

- "Courage! . . . It is I. Don't be afraid!" (Matthew 14:27)

- "I know my sheep and they know me." (John 10:14–15)

## Break Open Scripture at Home

In essence, whenever we talk about God's Word and what it means in our lives, we are doing a type of "breaking open the Word." We can always deepen our understanding of the Word by discussing it with others. Parents and children can grow in faith by reflecting together on the Word of God.

In chapter 9 of this guide, we detailed a method for you to use in "breaking open" Sunday Scripture with children. Parents can use a similar method at home or in the car on the way home from church, school, or religious education. Help parents to see that talking about Scripture does not have to be a big, formal, complicated process. Encourage parents to use a simplified version of breaking open Scripture by asking children these two questions:

- What did you hear?

- What did it mean?

Let's look at the purpose of these two simple questions, which can be asked anywhere!

**What did you hear?** Or, another way to ask the question might be, What was the Scripture story today? The purpose of this question is to allow the child to talk about the story. It really does not matter what words the adult uses; the point is to have the child tell the adult what he or she heard. The child may not even give an accurate depiction of the Scripture story but will tell what he or she heard.

For example, if the children heard the story "Peter Learns to Have Great Trust in Jesus" (Matthew 14:22–33; 19th Sunday in Ordinary Time, Year A), during lunch or on the drive home from school or Mass, the parent might ask, "What Scripture story did you hear today?" Often a child cannot remember what she or he heard, but after a little prompting, the child may respond in words like: "Jesus was walking on water. The Apostles thought he was a ghost." Then the parent would naturally follow up with something like: "What do you mean, 'Jesus was walking on water'? Tell me more." Such an exchange is an example of how a parent encourages the child to talk about what she or he heard. Then the parent moves the conversation to the second question.

**What did it mean?** Or, another way to ask this question is, What is God's message? The purpose of this question is to help the child grasp a message for life. In this example, the parent tries to lead the child to trust Jesus and turn to Jesus in times of trouble. Encourage parents to use the Understand It! panel of *The Catholic Children's Bible* as a resource for understanding various Scripture stories.

## Build a Bible Corner at Home

You probably have a Bible corner in your classroom, where you gather to pray and reflect upon the Word of God. Talk to your children about the importance of the Bible corner and suggest that they make a simple Bible corner at home. Be sure to tell them to talk to a parent about it first. And, remember, a Bible corner can be simple and temporary. In other words, it does not have to be a permanent fixture in the home. You can build it when you need it!

## Love It! Live It!

All in all, the most important thing you can do in sharing Scripture with families is to love and live the Gospel. You are already showing your commitment to the Gospel by being a catechist or a Catholic school teacher. Your students and their families look to you as a model of discipleship. Keep up the good work!

# Acknowledgments

The scriptural quotations in this publication are from the Good News Translation® (Today's English Version, Second Edition). Copyright © 1992 by the American Bible Society. All rights reserved. Bible text from the Good News Translation (GNT) is not to be reproduced in copies or otherwise by any means except as permitted in writing by the American Bible Society, 1865 Broadway, New York, NY 10023 (*www.americanbible. org*).

The quotations labeled *Catechism* and *CCC* are from the English translation of the *Catechism of the Catholic Church* for use in the United States of America, second edition. Copyright © 1994 by the United States Catholic Conference, Inc.—Libreria Editrice Vaticana (LEV). English translation of the *Catechism of the Catholic Church: Modifications from the Editio Typica* copyright © 1997 by the United States Catholic Conference, Inc.—LEV.

The quotations on pages 8 and 9 and the excerpt on pages 15–16 are from *The Word of the Lord (Verbum Domini)*, numbers 7, 16, and 42, at *www.vatican.va/holy_ father/benedict_xvi/apost_exhortations/documents/hf_ben-xvi_exh_20100930_verbum-domini_en.html*. Copyright © 2010 LEV.

The first excerpt on page 10 is from *National Directory for Catechesis*, by the United States Conference of Catholic Bishops (USCCB) (Washington, DC: USCCB, 2005), page 70. Copyright © 2005 USCCB, Washington, D.C. All rights reserved. No part of this work may be reproduced or transmitted in any form or by any means, electronic or mechanical, including photocopying, recording, or by any information storage and retrieval system, without permission in writing from the copyright holder.

The second excerpt on page 10 is from *Dogmatic Constitution on Divine Revelation* (*Dei Verbum*, 1965), number 25, in *Vatican Council II: Constitutions, Decrees, Declarations*, Austin Flannery, general editor (Northport, NY: Costello Publishing Company, 1996). Copyright © 1996 by Reverend Austin Flannery.

The words from the Mass on the handouts "Prayers for Palm / Passion Sunday" (Document #: TX003067) and "Prayers for the Triduum" (Document #: TX003068) are from the English translation of *The Roman Missal* © 2010, International Commission on English in the Liturgy Corporation (ICEL) (Washington, DC: United States Conference of Catholic Bishops, 2011), pages 532, 669, 532, and 648, respectively. Copyright © 2011, USCCB, Washington, D.C. All rights reserved. No part of this work may be reproduced or transmitted in any form or by any means, electronic or mechanical, including photocopying, recording, or by any information storage and retrieval system, without permission in writing from the copyright holder. Used with permission of the ICEL.

To view copyright terms and conditions for Internet materials cited here, log on to the home pages for the referenced Web sites.

During this book's preparation, all citations, facts, figures, names, addresses, telephone numbers, Internet URLs, and other pieces of information cited within were verified for accuracy. The authors and Saint Mary's Press staff have made every attempt to reference current and valid sources, but we cannot guarantee the content of any source, and we are not responsible for any changes that may have occurred since our verification. If you find an error in, or have a question or concern about, any of the information or sources listed within, please contact Saint Mary's Press.

### Endnote Cited in a Quotation from the *Catechism of the Catholic Church,* Second Edition

Chapter 2

1. *Dei Verbum* 25; cf. *Philippians* 3:8 and St. Jerome, *Commentariorum in Isaiam libri xviii* prol.: J. P. Migne, ed., Patrologia Latina (Paris: 1841–1855) 24, 17B.

### Endnote Cited in a Quotation from *Verbum Domini,* Number 42

Chapter 3

1. *Propositio* 29.